My Life in The Supernatural: A Story of Divine Mercy

(De Santiago Family Publishing)
ISBN-13: 978-0692891711
ISBN-10: 0692891714

For Juanito

Table of Contents

Chapter 1. The Beginning

My "life" began on March 22, 2006. It was the darkest of nights on that third day of Spring. That night though, which seemed to be the end of all my nights, would actually be the night of my rebirth.

I was born in the small town of Mineral Wells, Texas in 1972. My parents were both immigrants from Mexico. They had 7 children, with me being the youngest of 5 boys and 2 girls. I've lived in Mineral Wells my entire life with the exception of the 2 years that we lived in South Texas when I was very young. My father moved us all there in the mid-1970's to find a specialist for an injury that he received while working for a railroad company, where 2 of my uncles worked as well. During our 2 years in South Texas, my father made a living by picking oranges, peppers, and onions, like many migrant workers, did. On many occasions, he took the whole family out to help pick the various types of vegetables and fruits to gain more money, as he was paid by the load. I can still remember the smell of the orange trees as me and one my sisters played around them while ignoring our duties. The many subsequent trips to South Texas in the many years since living there, and seeing the orange trees, brings back memories of a simpler life.

My introduction to the supernatural began in those years living in South Texas. The 2 very profound memories from that time are still very clear to this day.

The first experience was at breakfast time on a school day. I was the only one of my siblings who was not in school yet. My brothers and sisters were around the kitchen table eating that early morning in our very small and poor house. I was in my mother's arms, and I saw an image moving on the small square window on the battered door that led to the outside. I was somewhat afraid, but my very young mind was use to seeing things of this nature then, although I only remember these 2 incidences now.

The second and most frightening incident occurred in the dead of night. Given our poverty-leveled lifestyle, all of our family, except my paternal grandmother, who slept in a closet that was turned into a bedroom, slept in one bedroom. My brothers and sister slept side by side on the floor, while I slept on the bed next to my mother and father. I remember looking out of the bedroom window as something had awakened me. What I saw, scared me to death. I was only 3 or 4 years old at the time but the image is ingrained in my memory to this day. The dark figure had the shape of what most people think about when they think of a witch. The whole pointed hat, pointed nose, and pointed chin type of caricature. I screamed at the top of my lungs, which woke everyone up. I cried and cried uncontrollably. I tried to explain to everyone what I had just seen, and I remember that my mom, gave me aspirin to try to calm me down and to get me back to sleep. I can only imagine what my brothers and sisters thought of that whole incident at the time.

My mom later said, that they took me to what Mexicans call, a "curandero", which is something like a witch doctor. He did a ritual to try to cleanse me or some nonsense like that, of whatever I was suffering from. Looking back, all these years later, I believe what I experienced was of a demonic nature. What I've been given to experience since 2006, solidifies that notion.

The rest of my childhood and that of my years growing up were somewhat normal. I do consider it though, that I did have a happy childhood. Even though we were poor, I was happy.

I did have the sporadic prophetic dreams in between those early years until that fateful night on March 22, 2006. Dreams of what was going to come to pass, specifically the physical growth of my small town. Dreams of stores and shops and businesses and their exact future locations came to be. I would relate these dreams to my mom, and then when they came to pass after some time, she reminded me of what I had told her. It was just a curious thing to me, but nothing more than that.

That early Spring night in 2006, was the tipping point of my life which was slowly building up from my 20's through my very early 30's. Like most young men, I wanted a career, family, success, all the things that this world deems to be what life is all about. Even though I was church-going Catholic, I had no relationship with God. That void, I tried to fill with so many things that were not of Him. My only thought of the afterlife was that of Hell and my fear of going to Hell.

The details that led to that March night, is not of importance at this time. The only thing that needs to be known, is that I thought that God hated me, that He had it out for me. In the Fall of 2005, I thought the tide finally began to turn in my favor. There was a girl, who was a family friend, whom I began to have feelings for after some time of getting to know her better. I had known her for a while, but I hadn't really paid her no mind, till she started to pay attention to me.

On New Year's Eve of 2005, I went to a gathering at our church to bring in the New Year with the Charismatic Prayer Group that my father started in 1986 after his powerful conversion. The only reason I went, was because this girl was going to be there. The temporary priest we had at the time, was an Indian priest. His name was Father Jerome. This older priest was very kind. He was there that night in our small parish hall with the Group. We were all joking around with him and I don't remember what I said, but it was something jokingly about his age, perhaps because he immediately asked me how old I was. I answered, "I'm 33". Father Jerome replied "33?! By the time Jesus was 33, He had already been in His ministry for multiple years. What have you done?" Everyone that was around Father Jerome, laughed including the girl. I remember very clearly that my first thought when he had said that was, "my time has not yet come". I don't why I thought that, but little did I know that my first vision, a vision of death, was less than six months away and my life would be changed forever.

I lost all hope after this friendship, attempted relationship with this girl, went south. I was crushed. The proverbial straw that broke the camel's back had arrived. The culmination of everything that happened from my 20's to that fateful night, peaked. I thought of taking my own life but the thought of my mother and the fear of going to Hell stopped me from doing that. I felt that I had lost everything, and all that I saw and felt, was darkness. I felt like I was losing my mind. I felt that I was losing control of reality. As I sat at the edge of my bed, I took my phone out, and I started to type out a message, a message to God.

I typed out everything that I was feeling, and I asked God, "Why are You doing this to me? Why do you keep punishing me? Why do you hate me? I can't do this anymore? If You're going to help me, then help me!". I don't remember how I fell asleep that night but I do remember, that I dreaded getting up the next couple of days.

A few days later, I went online, and I went to the Catholic website EWTN. I specifically went to the question and answer section, like I did on occasion. In this particular forum, Catholic experts, including priests, would answer questions that were submitted. Even though I was a nominal Catholic, I still was very interested in the different types of Catholic subjects. This particular header got my attention on this day. It read, "vision of Hell". As I described earlier, Hell was a subject I was very interested in, because I was so afraid of it. I don't remember the exact question, but in this message, this person copied and pasted an excerpt from Saint Faustina's experience, about her vision of Hell. It fascinated me, but it also scared me even more about Hell. I immediately searched some more about this Saint Faustina, and I found out that this excerpt, was from her diary, from her book. The book was "Diary: Divine Mercy In My Soul"

Saint Maria Faustina Kowalska was a Polish Catholic nun from the 1930's who had incredible visions, and apparitions of our Lord Jesus Christ, the Holy Virgin Mary, and many other Heavenly visitors, including many demonic apparitions and visions as well. I immediately ordered the book the next day. The message of Divine Mercy changed my life. It seemed like the book was written specifically for me. I began to understand that God wasn't punishing me, He was calling me to Himself, but I wasn't listening. This burning desire to save souls began in my own soul. I went to confession after 11 years and very quickly, that darkness that had invaded my soul for so many years, turned into light. I was so fascinated with the fact that the Lord Jesus, could show a human being such incredible things. I felt I received a clean slate and new beginning with the Plenary Indulgence that I gained through the Feast of Divine Mercy that came the first Sunday after Easter. This was just 6 weeks or so after that dark March night.

I began to pray for other people. That was something that I really had not done before. One of the prayers, that I began to pray, was the Chaplet of Divine Mercy which I learned from the "Diary" of Saint Faustina. A couple of the promises attached in praying the Chaplet of Divine Mercy are, if the most hardened sinner was to recite this chaplet once, the Lord will grant him a grace from His infinite mercy. One of the other promises that Jesus told Saint Faustina about the Chaplet, is that if the chaplet is recited for the dying, the Lord Jesus promised that He Himself would stand between the dying person and God the Father not as a just judge, but as a merciful Savior. The second promise for the dying is that Jesus would grant Mercy at the hour of death of the dying person. Saint Faustina wrote multiple stories of her recitation of the chaplet for the dying. It was fascinating. I found information online on how people had ministries of praying for the dying. People would go to those who were near death in hospitals, hospices or wherever they were, and prayed this chaplet of mercy, this Chaplet of Divine Mercy for their souls. That was something I wanted to do.

I struggled after that first confession after 11 years. I wound up going to confession six weeks in a row to get rid of everything that I felt I had. I suffered from scrupulosity I later found out, I thought every little bad thing that entered my mind or some little bad deed that I did, that I felt was offending God, I felt that I needed to go to confession. I struggled with scrupulosity for a while.

I was happy for the first time in a very long while. I was receiving Jesus in the Holy Eucharist with clean heart and soul and mind. I wanted to spread God's message of mercy to everyone with this fire that seemed to be lit in my soul. I ended up purchasing another copy of the "Diary" for the girl. I felt it was God's will for me to do so.

We got a new young priest in our Parish in the second month of my conversion and I met with him to ask him about God's Will.

It was a little surreal as I entered his office to speak with him because I never imagined I would be speaking to a priest about such things. His office was the old residence of our beloved Irish priest Father Nagle, who was our pastor for 50 years in our small town. The memories of my childhood growing up in our church, seemed to come back as I entered the office. The memories of catechism classes, Easter egg hunt's, and

Vacation Bible School, seemed like it was only yesterday.

After the usual pleasantries, I asked him what God's will was. The young priest answered, "if there's good that comes from it, then you know it's God's will", and with that, I left with the conviction that I had to give this girl a copy of the "Diary".

I received the new copy of the book from an online superstore and I was excited. "I am doing God's will!" my renewed soul proclaimed. I wrapped it in some plain wrapping paper and I gave the girl the "Diary" after the Spanish Mass. She thanked me and went on her way.

Chapter 2. June 28, 2006.

Three months and five days after that dark night, things were still getting better. I started to pray more, but not for myself, but for other people. I felt that praying for myself, made me feel selfish, but I guess that's typical in new conversions. One feels like we don't deserve anything from God, when we look back on the type of life we led prior to our conversions. As time went on though, I did start to pray for myself.

I was working in the afternoon on June 27, 2006, in our family business. We have a janitorial service and carpet cleaning service, which my family started about 30 years earlier. The job-site we were working at was an antenna manufacturing company which is across this popular fast food chicken place in our small town. There was nothing strange about that day until we got to that job- site that late afternoon. I was vacuuming in this two-story building when I started feeling something. It felt like an uneasiness in my soul. It was very distinct because the peace that I had, was disturbed. I just dismissed it though.

On June 28th, once again there was nothing strange about that day. We arrived that late afternoon to the same antenna-manufacturing site as part of our daily workday. Again, I was vacuuming, and this disturbance started just like the day before but this time it was a lot stronger. I remembered from St Faustina's Diary, that she had similar experiences. When she would feel these "disturbances", she would pray and ask God, to be given to know what she was feeling. I thought, "I'm going to do the same thing!". So at that moment, I began to pray so that God would show me what I was feeling. I prayed the Holy Rosary. I had been praying the Rosary every day since my conversion started and so I thought this would be the perfect prayer for that Grace. After I finished the final prayer, it seemed like my mind was being hijacked. It felt like someone had taken control of my thoughts. My eyes were closed and I could see images being flashed in my mind's eye. It was not just images that were being flashed, but there were feelings associated with it as well. They were feelings of pain, sorrow, and suffering and a distinct sense of death as well. It all freaked me out needless to say. I was overwhelmed. "What just happened?" I thought to myself. At the next job-site, the public library, I told my mom what had just happened. She had experience in things like this because of her many years in the Charismatic Prayer movement as I talked about earlier. She said that I had just received a vision. The vision I had was of the girl, whom I talked about earlier, and it was somehow related to death, the death of a child.

The girl had gotten pregnant a few months earlier by a friend of hers, who was now her boyfriend. At this point, I had no feelings for her at all, which I found somewhat strange after what I felt for her just some months earlier. That night, my mom ended up praying for me along with my sister, trying to calm me of what I had just experienced just a couple of hours earlier.

I tried to understand why I received this vision. I prayed for answers. I was hoping in a way, that my mom would invite me to the prayer meeting that they had every Thursday in the church hall. I asked God "if it is Your will, let my mom invite me to the prayer meeting so I may receive an answer, to why I received this vision". A couple of days later, my mom invited me to the prayer meeting and again I was excited because I knew God had answered my prayer.

I was a little nervous as that first prayer meeting began. I sat in an old folded metal chair which looked like it been there for ages. Our new priest showed up as well. I believe he was trying to get acclimated with all the church groups and so he paid us a visit that night. He sat right next to me. The praise and worship music began, as it was the format that had been established long before my arrival. I joined in as best as I could hiding my nervousness. The time arrived when the Holy Spirit was invoked and the deeper prayer began. We all held hands. We all were asked to close our eyes. The music had slowed to a pace, which set the tone for this type of prayer. The type of music where the words and beat move your soul to a heavenly place. Almost immediately I felt something. It was like this electricity started from one end of my hand, and then went up my arm and then down my spine and then all the way up again and then down through my other arm. At that moment, I received my second vision. It was of a dark nature, symbols of death, or at least that's how I discerned it at the time. The vision, had a darker than night background with a long wooden staff right in the middle and a large snake slithering its way around making its way to the top. The final image of this, was that of a baby. It frightened me. I immediately connected it to the first vision. This put more on edge than before. I believe from that second vision, God opened the floodgates to this supernatural world. It seemed like the veil that separates the natural and supernatural, was lifted from me. This new world was opened up before me. I began experiencing all sorts of spiritual things. I started feeling darkness around people, places, and around all sorts of things. I started seeing dark shadows moving about as I closed my eyes to pray as well. These "shadows", always came with a terrible feeling, which felt like nothing I had ever felt before. I was given to know through prayer and through endless questions, and through tons of research, that these "shadows" were evil spirits, fallen angels, demons. They are all the same. This early period turned my life inside out and upside down. I was a mess, that peace which I enjoyed for a short time, was long gone. My prayer life increased as the darkness increased. The Lord God guided me with His Spirit, to certain Saints to help me through this early period. First, it was Saint Padre Pio of Pietrelcina, the 20th Century Capuchin priest. Then it was Saint Therese of Lisieux, and then to Saint Gemma Galgani. In reading of the lives of these Saints, a lot of my answers came. I realized that there were many people in which God worked in the way He began working in me. These great Saints became my best friends, in particular Padre Pio. Reading about his life left me in wonderment. Along with the Saints, my mother helped me tremendously. She had been through her own mystical path and she was able to understand some of what I was going through. She calmed my nerves more than I can count, especially those days when the demonic presences were more than I could handle. I also received help from this mystery woman from Australia through a Catholic online forum. She posted about some similar experiences like I was going through. I ended up private messaging her. We communicated for about two weeks and she was able to help me put names to these things I was experiencing. They were spiritual gifts from God. She had attended a spiritual gifts workshop in her parish in Australia, and so she was familiar with all these things. She was also the one that helped me to understand that I shouldn't be afraid of these dark evil spirits, she told me I was protected. From that moment, I ceased being afraid. Mysteriously, after two weeks of contact with this woman, I never heard from her again. I truly believe God put her in my path to help me. It was a God send as some people call it.

After a couple of weeks, I began to discern that this vision had a secondary purpose to it. It was not only a vision of death, but also, that this vision had to be relayed to the person involved, the "girl". This seemed like an impossible task at first. How was I supposed to tell a pregnant woman that I had a vision of the death of her unborn child? I then started having dreams about this vision as well. One in particular, was of the girl in an operating room with a doctor wearing the typical green surgical scrubs. He had finished some type of procedure or some type of operation on her. He then walks towards me and shows me both his hands which were covered with an incredible amount of blood. These dreams to me, was further confirmation of this vision being true. I told some people I trusted about what I had been given to discern about all this, the vision and the "message". All across the board, it was received like something that they never had to deal with before. I even reached out to a well-known Charismatic Renewal priest for advice via email, and he was neutral on the whole thing. I just continued to pray on it all as I couldn't get an answer one way or another. After a lot of prayer, I felt that the Lord was telling me "yes", to relaying the vision and message to the girl. I asked for a sign from God through Saint Therese's intercession to be 100% sure. I received my sign in the form a rose, which is typical of St. Therese. After that, I had no doubt. I knew what I had to do. Now it was just a matter of getting together with the girl and telling her the vision and message. It had been something like 4 or 5 weeks worth of praying by the time the day arrived for me to tell her the vision.

It was a Thursday when I messaged her letting her know that I needed to talk to her about something very important. We agreed to meet around 8pm. That night we also had another prayer meeting, and that night, some of the group prayed over me. I received further confirmation from one of the people praying over me, that what I had to do just a bit later, was the will of God.

I left right before the prayer meeting ended, and I met the girl at a local high school parking lot just outside the running track. It was a typical midsummer night in Texas, the sounds of crickets off in distance could be heard along with the faint sound of conversations coming from the dozen or so people on the track. After a slightly awkward greeting, we sat on the tailgate of the truck that she arrived in. I then proceeded to tell her everything that had happened since everything went south between us just 4 months earlier. I then confidently went into the whole reason of being there, the vision and message. I described it with as much detail as possible, being sure to not forget any part of it. I told her that the situation between her and I, was God's Providence. He had used her to finally reach me, and now, He was using me to reach her. Her life at that point wasn't what one would call being faithful to the Church's teachings on many fronts. I will just leave it at that. Her reaction to the whole "vision", was a total surprise to me. It was just a "thank you for telling me" and, "I have to go home and get some rest". I left bewildered. Had she not believed anything I had just told her? I got home and told some of my family what had transpired. I know I had done what I was supposed to do in telling her the vision and message. Right before I went to bed though, I received this "understanding" that she did indeed believe what I told her on this late July night. I went to sleep with this renewed peace. I woke up that next day with a peace, that surpassed anything that I had felt before in my life.

The morning after, I went to work and the peace I went to sleep with, seemed to be increasing as the day went on. I was truly happy for the first time in forever it seemed like. I kept thanking God for allowing me to have this incredible peace after what seemed to be an eternity of darkness. I took a nap after lunch as I regularly do, because of our work schedule. Our mornings have always consisted of carpet cleaning and our late afternoon and evenings, were dedicated to our janitorial services. When I woke up from my nap, the peace that had enveloped me was gone. What replaced it, was a disturbance but it was a little different from what I had experienced up to that point. It felt like someone wanted to do me harm, like someone had this need, this urge, to try to hurt me. This was an infused understanding of what this feeling was. I began to pray as we started our work in the early afternoon, and this feeling just kept building and building till it finally peaked and I recognized that it was an evil spirit that was behind it. When this feeling peaked, I was in this PVC pipe factory restroom by myself and all of a sudden, the door of the bathroom stall slammed shut by itself and this terrible feeling I had left, and this incredible peace that I had woken up to returned. I was a little perplexed in the beginning to what had just happened. I checked to see if it wasn't the air from the vent above in this old and very out of date restroom that closed this door shut. It wasn't the air or any other natural force that made this grayish stall door slam shut. It was an evil spirit which was trying to scare me for some reason, or perhaps it was showing its anger that I had not fallen back to who I was before. Who knows, but I thanked God for it. To me, it was just more confirmation that God had begun working through me and in a very powerful and supernatural way.

After that day, my real work began, that is, the work that would become my life. The work of praying for souls.

The next day or so these "soul disturbances", became more frequent and always, it was accompanied by a vision and with an understanding of what or who needed to be prayed for. It seemed like clockwork that when this work was completed, the disturbance left and the peace returned. It was truly like a floodgate that had opened up in my life.

As the days and weeks and months went by, the Spirit of the Lord opened up more spiritual gifts within me. I started to feel the conditions of people's souls and at times, I could see it as well. That made it hard for me in the beginning, to be around people. Going to the grocery store or even to restaurants became such a heavy burden on me. As soon as I would walk into one of these public places, I began to feel everybody and everything. It was like I couldn't shut off this "noise". The "noise" of souls being filled with things of this world and not of things of God. I started to avoid going to places where there were large amounts of people. I could even feel and hear the "noise" at mass on Sundays.

As part of our work, our carpet cleaning service, we went to many homes throughout my hometown and surrounding towns nearby. In some of these houses, I could tell when someone had died in that particular house. It seems a little awkward to me now, but I would always ask the customer in some sort of way the history of the house, mainly the deaths that had occurred and always, I was correct in what I was given to see and to know and to feel. On more than one occasion, I went around certain houses rebuking the evil spirits that seemed to be lingering about in which the customers chalked up as being "ghosts".

All the while, the first vision of the girl was never far from my mind. She was getting very close to her due date. It was just about a month away now. Then came a moment that changed my life once more, and this time it would be what became my greatest gift from God.

Chapter 3. The Hises

In mid-October of 2006, our parish had our annual Jamaica celebration. The Jamaica was started by our old Irish priest Father John Nagle many years ago. It is the church's biggest fundraiser, which features many booths of authentic Mexican food and traditional Mexican music and dances. It has many games for the kids as well. The Jamaica has provided many fond memories for me and my family who have participated in it on a yearly basis. This particular year, it was the first time they held it in the church parking lot. In the previous years, it had been held out in the old military base, which had another Catholic Church, in which our old Irish priest celebrated mass there as well many moons ago.

Part of that 2006's Jamaica, a silent auction took place. My family's carpet cleaning service offered some cleaning as part of our donation. A couple of days later, we got a call from someone who had won the auction for our services, and so we set up the appointment for the following Saturday, exactly a week after the Jamaica.

That fateful Saturday, my oldest sister and I, went to this new housing development just outside of town which is right by the old military base.

The Fort Wolters military base, during World War II, was for a time the largest infantry replacement-training center in the United States. After the war, it became an

Air Force base. One of the most decorated American combat soldiers of World War II, Audie Murphy, completed his basic training there.

As we entered the fairly new built house, the fresh smell of homemade flour tortillas filled the air. Memories of walking into my family's home and smelling the sweet aroma of fresh tortillas quickly filled my mind. Mrs. Hise had learned as she told us, when we inquired on where she learned this Mexican food mainstay, in South Texas where she grew up around Mexican friends and neighbors. She offered us some, but we politely declined since we had just come from our own breakfast a little earlier. Mr. Hise, a recently retired school administrator, conversed with us as we went about our work throughout the house. I noticed that on the coffee table, as I was moving about some of the furniture, that there was a small stack of aviation magazines. Mr. Hise proceeded to tell us that he was a pilot and now that he had more time on his hands, it would be spent golfing and flying. This newly developed housing area also had a country club and golf course adjacent to it. Then per usual, I received a disturbance in my soul. We were about to finish the last room of cleaning when this occurred. I told my sister what I was feeling. I told her that this feeling couldn't be with this nice couple, meaning the condition of their souls. Their hospitality towards us didn't seem to fit the feeling I was receiving from Above. My sister said that perhaps it was the helicopter crashes that took place decades earlier at the Air Force Base behind the Hise's home. There were several fatalities that took place there. I agreed with her, and I quickly said a prayer for the couple and for whatever else I was feeling. I also remember that I prayed to Saint Michael the Archangel for protection as well. We finished up our work and we said our good-byes and we left.

Saturday, November 11th, 2006, 3 weeks after the job for Mr. and Mrs. Hise, began like any other Saturday. There was a trip planned to a shopping mall in Fort Worth, that my sisters and my mom were going go to, to do some early Christmas shopping. I decided to tagalong. I was a little nervous because it was going to be a first time that I was going to be around a lot of people since this "life" of mine began. The thought of me "picking up" all sorts of things from people there, made me hesitate but I decided to go anyway. The whole time at the mall was uneventful till the very end. As we were walking out through one of the side exits, I gently bumped into a young girl dressed in all black. She was dressed like a typical Goth girl, black baggy denim jeans, a black shirt, and a black leather jacket and her hair was dark as well. The split second after that brief contact, I felt the condition of her soul, I felt all of the dark stuff that she had done up to that point in her life. It was like all of her sins and of her dark secrets were transferred to me. I felt awful needless to say. It took me about 30 minutes of constant prayer on the ride back home, to pray all this darkness away from my soul. I prayed for her soul as well. Then just like that, everything left and I was like I was before, at peace. That was the first time making physical contact with somebody, that the Lord God allowed me to "feel" someone and to "know" their condition of their soul by just by mere contact.

I got home and I went to the computer room. I went online to browse the usual sites. Browsing the news, the sports pages and my usual rundown of many Catholic sites, seemed to be my norm for me at that point. Despite trying to busy myself online, I was still thinking about what had occurred just an hour earlier with the Goth girl, when another disturbance hit my soul. The feeling I received was stronger than anything I had felt up to that point, but what accompanied that feeling I will never forget. It was screams of a woman, a woman in great pain and in great fear. I immediately got up and tried to find the source of the screams. I went to the living room to see if it was coming from the TV and it wasn't from there. I went to the nearby rooms and it wasn't coming from there either. I went back to my computer and the screams were piercing my soul now. I covered my ears and I could still hear the suffering cries of pain. This shook me to my very core to such a degree, that I had to leave my house and just drive. I drove to the church and I just sat in my car crying. I took out my Rosary out and I prayed a Chaplet of Mercy for whatever it was I was experiencing. I don't remember how I got back home or what happened the rest of that day.

The next morning we receive a call from a family friend, who was a fellow prayer group member, and she tells us the tragic news. The Hises had died in a plane crash the day before. They flew down to South Texas in their small plane to see some family and were returning back home when their plane went down short of our small hometown airport. It was a very gruesome scene we were told. Right then, it all hit me, the disturbance the day before, the screams of a woman, the disturbance that day at their house just a few weeks earlier, it was this, their death. What I received that day at their house, was their impending death. I was stunned. I relayed all this to my family and to the family friend who gave us the horrible news. They were all equally stunned. My mother then said to me that all of this, the visions and everything that I had been receiving from God, was for real. The look on her face when she told me this, was one of non-comprehension of the magnitude of what had just occurred with her youngest child.

Shortly after at morning mass, we met the family friend who passed along the news, and at that point, I felt this sadness that was so deep, that it hurt my soul. The gravity of the whole situation hit me hard. I thought that I hadn't prayed enough for them before their death. I couldn't get them off of my mind for a long while after that. Every time I gave testimony about it, even years after it occurred, I would tear up and feel the pain all over again. I've offered masses for them in the years since their deaths. I know with every bit of my being, that God had mercy on them. This is still the one of the most painful of all the experiences I have received and there's been a ton of them.

About a month after the Hise's death, the "girl" gave birth to a healthy child. It made me doubt for a minute, the first vision. Was it a false vision? Was it my mind? Why did God allow me to go through so much grief over it? So many questions and emotions filled my mind and soul. In the days and months after I told the girl the vision, I fervently prayed for it not to come to pass. Her family went everywhere asking for prayers as well. Did God answer all these prayers? I know that God did not allow my conversion, this particular path that He had me on now, to start on a false premise, especially with something so delicate as this. After the Hise's death, I thought it further confirmed to me that first vision of death. My other sister helped calm my nerves that day of the birth. She reminded me of all the other things that God had allowed me by His Grace to do, to experience, to pray for. This did humble me. I was reminded that God's plans were far greater than my small mind could comprehend. The strange thing about this, is that for several years after the birth, I still felt death with the girl and her child. Was the vision a future event that will still come to pass? Only God knows. I still pray for her and family as part of my daily prayers.

Chapter 4. Dreams

I felt an inspiration to journal everything I was experiencing very early on in my conversion. It was great therapy for me in those early years. Leaving everything on the pages was a big help in my formation. It was still a lot for me to carry, but it was made easier by journaling.

May of 2007, was another turning point in my life. As part of my journaling in 2006, I began writing down some of my dreams. I had some very profound dreams in 2006. During the early months of my conversion, during the period where my fear of the evil spirits was at its peak, the evilness crossed over into my dreams. I would wake up with such a fear like I've never experienced before. The feeling would linger long after I would wake up. The Heavenly aspect of the dreams was just as profound.

While we were at one of our janitorial jobs, an old Catholic Hospital that was converted to social services building, early on mid-May morning, I went out to throw the trash away in the dumpster. When I opened up the old rusted lid, I looked what was on the inside, and there was a cross-country ski machine that was all the rage just a decade earlier. At that moment, I had a flashback to a dream I had just some nights earlier in which I wrote down in my journal. The thrown away cross-country ski machine was mostly made out of wood, with some parts metal. The wooden skis were medium brown and varnished. When I got home later that morning, I brought out my journal, and I flipped back several pages, and I saw where I had written down where I dreamed of the exact same ski machine, down to the exact medium brown varnished skis. In the dream, I was in a storage facility that was full of junk and behind the door, was the ski machine. I remember clearly that in the dream, I was on my knees pushing the junk out of my way as I crawled towards the door. I just stared at the machine just observing all the details of it for some reason. The machines became scarce by 2006, or at least in my view they were, because I had not seen one in quite a while. Seeing this dream, or these details come to pass fascinated me. From that point, these prophetic dreams came fast and steady. I started to put more details in my journal about all the dreams that I had, and so when things would come to pass, I would revert back to the journals and show people how my dreams were coming true. I guess this was some sort of validation for me to show others, on what I was receiving from God, was in fact true. I would dream of everything, from places I was yet to visit, to people that I've yet to meet, to even the smallest most insignificant detail of something within the dream, it would all came to pass.

The significance of these dreams became somehow more real to me, when I had dreamed of a person and that person ended up dying shortly after. I would dream of a person for example, that I had not seen in years, and then I would read about or somehow the news got back to me, that the person died just days after I had dreamed of them. Almost immediately, I would pray the Chaplet of Divine Mercy for whoever I had just dreamed about. After a while, I knew if I dreamed of a specific person, it also meant I had to pray for their families as well because whatever was going to occur, there was a good chance it was about their families too. My dreams had become another part of my "job" now. My sleep became burdensome at times because I tried really hard to remember every little dream I had because I knew it was of importance. I would wake up in the middle of the night and write down whatever I had just dreamed, I would write them down on whatever piece of paper I could find. I have many notes written down on a ton of store receipts.

Two of the dreams in particular that I had early on, were pretty similar in theme. Both were of high school classmates whom I had not seen since graduation some 15 years earlier or so at the time.

The first one was of a classmate who I also received First Communion with, when we were both small and in the second grade. He was just someone I knew by the time that we both graduated from high school, so it wasn't a friendship or anything like that. In the dream, I'm standing in a schoolyard and a group of kids run by me really quick, and within this group, this classmate stops right in front of me and just stops and just stares at me for about five seconds and then he takes off running again. The odd thing about this was that he was dressed like a priest. A few days or so after the dream, I read in our local newspaper, in the obituaries, that this classmate's mother just passed away. The obituary read that she was attending a church that was not Catholic at the time of her death. The Lord God once again allowed me to pray for mercy upon her soul before she passed. I'm not sure why the Lord allowed me to "see" and pray for this particular death. I honestly cannot remember the last time I had talked to

this classmate. The only two connections I had were our First Communion, and our high school graduation. God's mercy is way beyond my comprehension but I know He had mercy on her soul.
The second dream was pretty similar to the first dream. In this dream, I was in our chapel and I was walking out and I noticed this second classmate just standing there towards the back, behind all the wooden pews in this 70 plus-year-old rock structured church. I walk past him and he just looks at me with an expressionless look on his face. I just stare back and I just walk away. I made a connection to the first classmate with that expressionless look on both their faces. Once again like before, I see in the obituaries a few days later, that this second classmate's aunt had just died. Once again like before, the Lord God granted me the grace to pray for mercy for her soul. Praise be to God!

This list of people whom the Lord has granted me to pray for through my dreams is far more than I can count now.

There are times when the person in my dream, is the person who is going to die. Like the time I was shown a death list in my dream and at the bottom of that list, was one of my uncles from Mexico. A couple of days later, he died but I know in my heart once again, God had mercy on him because He allowed me to pray for mercy for him before he passed away. In the case of my uncle and others, some of these souls had strayed from God and the Church. I believe great Mercy was granted to them because of prayers on their behalf from someone, mostly likely from family.

The one thing about dreams, is that one has to have discernment on them because sometimes, dreams are just dreams and nothing more. I learned that the hard way. At one time I believed that whatever I dreamed, was from God. I tried to force situations in real life to fit the dream because I wholeheartedly believed that it was from God. Needless to say, those situations went south very fast. I do know, that when I do dream of death, it's a very likely that a death will occur and will occur very soon.

When God wants to show me something or wants me to pray for something, it doesn't matter what day it is, or what I'm doing, or whatever is going on in my life, He is going to bring it to me no matter what the occasion.

On my birthday in 2007, I decided to go to Fort Worth to go shopping at a sports superstore. It was a Saturday and I had no work to do that day. I had some birthday money that was given to me the day before from some my family. I remember feeling good that morning because it was my birthday first of all, and secondly, I had money in my pocket. Right before I arrived at the sports store from the 45-minute drive from my hometown, this disturbance hit my soul. I was getting pretty good at discerning when this death feeling was coming and sure enough, this was one of them. The reason this death feeling is so distinct is because in those early days, it felt like a piece of me was dying. It felt like my soul was being torn out of my chest, ripped to shreds, beat up, thrashed or however way possible a soul can be dismantled, it felt like that. It is by far the worst feeling. I do not know if these adjectives do justice to the way it feels.

As I got to the parking lot of the sports store, I just sat there in my yellow mustang convertible totally enveloped in this feeling of death. I gathered myself and I prayed the Chaplet of Divine Mercy for whose ever death was about to occur. I remember walking the aisles of the store with tear stained cheeks and thinking "all these people here have no idea what I have just experienced". I felt like such an outcast at that moment. Here these people were just enjoying their Saturday morning shopping and there I was with my soul in pieces. A couple of days later or so I happened to walk by as a TV was broadcasting the local news. They were showing security footage of a robbery in East Dallas. The armed gunman in this video was wearing a blue hoodie as he robbed and shot and killed this convenient store clerk. If there was ever a feeling of déjà vu, this was it. I know I had just seen this scene somewhere, and so I went quickly to my bedroom and brought out my journal. I found exactly what I had just seen on TV. I described the gruesome scene exactly down to the blue hoodie of the murderer from a dream I had on my birthday. I connected it all quickly, the sports store, the disturbance, the death feeling that morning, this was it. Little did I know that when I wrote that dream down, before I took off to that sports store on my birthday, that this was going to be a death that was going to happen some 14 or 15 hours later. Evil did not win that day, God had mercy on this East Dallas clerk's soul. To this day, I do not even know his name.

These prophetic dreams were at times perplexing. I would dream of the most insignificant thing that would come to pass and it had no rhyme or reason for it. It was just something that I saw in a dream that came to pass in real life. This occurs quite frequently. I would ask people what they thought of this and it came to two different schools of thought. The first one, that they were signs from God that He was still working through me through dreams. The second school of thought was that it's just part of the gift that I was given. I believe it's a combination of both.

Around the time that all the dreams started, I received this powerful vision during our prayer meeting one Thursday night. It started right when we got to the deep prayer part of the prayer meeting when we invoke the Holy Spirit. In the vision, the backdrop was a big wooded area and in front of that was an open field. I see two horses galloping towards me from this open field but they were galloping in slow motion. I see the horses getting closer, and I see that the horses were pale in color and on top, was this dark, black, jagged edge figure riding it. It was a very frightful site. I had to open my eyes for a bit because of the fear I had but when I closed them again, the vision was still there and these dark riders were getting closer to me. I just stopped praying and I opened my eyes trying to figure out what I had just seen. I knew this vision represented death because it felt like death. It wasn't until a couple of months later, when we were having Bible study with my parents at the house, that I came upon the book of Revelation 6:8, "I looked, and there before me was a pale horse! Its rider was named Death, and Hades was following close behind him. They were given power over a fourth of the earth to kill by sword, famine and plague, and by the wild beasts of the earth.". The Lord God had confirmed to me through the Holy Bible, that this vision was indeed of death, and that I truly had been given the gift of seeing death before it came, in order to pray for these souls, to pray for mercy for them. There was a sense of relief when I received this confirmation. Thanks be to God! The visions of death through my dreams became a regular occurrence.

Chapter 5. More Visions of Death

In early 2010 I was diagnosed with diabetes. I fasted on Ash Wednesday like we're required to do and so I woke up the next morning to weigh myself and I noticed that I had lost 5 pounds. My weight had been rock steady for quite a long time. I was very active and running at the track and on a treadmill multiple times a week and eating somewhat healthy and so this was a surprise. After I had lost another pound or so, my mom got worried and wanted me to go get some blood work done and so I did. I admit that I was a little worried at first. I went to the mobile health clinic that was parked in our middle school parking lot and I got my blood work done. I was really nervous for the next couple of days since the results took that long for them to come back. Prior to this, the Lord would let me know somehow or someway when an illness was coming to me, even like for the smallest thing like a cold. I had not received anything from Him about some illness coming my way and that's why I was nervous. So a couple of days went by and after work that Saturday morning after, I went to the lab at the hospital and I got a copy of my lab results. I asked the lab technician about what was on the lab report and he just said, "don't worry, you're not going to die" and with that, I had a little relief with that. The only abnormal thing about the results was that of my blood sugar and my A1C test, which indicated that I was diabetic. I went to the clinic at the hospital the next week and they put me on medication and gave me a list of things that I could not eat. I was overwhelmed with the suddenness of all this. I didn't realize that when I got the blood work done, that I had all the signs of diabetes, the excessive thirst, the excessive urination and the weight-loss. This was a test of my faith to say the least. I struggled with this disease mightily early on. I went to healing masses, I received the Sacrament of Anointing of the Sick from our new parish priest Father Balaji, and I prayed constantly for my healing.

Father B, as we call him, is an Indian priest from the Pallotine order. He is the most spiritual of all of the priests that have been here at our parish in my small town, after our long time Irish priest had retired and passed away. Our parish went through four priests in about 10 years before we received Father B.

In the numerous nights of praying for healing with my parents after I got sick, I received another powerful vision from Above in midst of one of those nights. The prayer session started like all the rest. I was, along with my parents, praying with much fervor for my healing when the vision started. In the vision, I was standing in a sea of people coming towards me and then past me as I stood still. The vision came with an understanding that all these people were the ones the Lord was going to allow me to see their impending deaths and be given the Grace to pray for mercy for them before they passed. There were many souls that I saw, I became overwhelmed at the sight of this. I began to weep at the magnitude of it all, and because of the feeling of all these upcoming deaths. This feeling of death accompanied the vision. I saw men and women of all ages pass by me. It was an endless stream of them. That vision has come true. The sheer number of deaths that I've been given to see since that powerful night has been staggering. Praise be to God and His Mercy!

After many prayers, this disease is still with me 6 years later. I submit to God's will on this. If it's His will for my complete healing on this, then may He be praised. If it's not His will, then may He be praised.

During the Christmas season in late 2008, I was at a Posada. A Posada is part of the traditional Mexican Christmas celebration. It is a reenactment of the census pilgrimage to Bethlehem by Mary and Joseph in search of a room. It's a multiple night celebration in which it's held at different houses each night. In the last part of the reenactment, the Rosary is prayed before a small model of the Nativity Scene. It was at this moment while praying the Rosary with many people in attendance, that the disturbance came. At first, I thought it was the condition of someone's soul that was very dark. The Spanish youth group from our parish had shown up and it seemed like some of them had been drinking prior to arriving at the Posada. My first thought was that it was one of them until I received a vision. The vision was of 2 black horses that were side by side galloping. All I saw was the base of their necks and up to their heads. The lines of the horse's figures were somewhat irregular. It was like they were drawn with some type of charcoal medium. I knew this was death, 2 to be exact. It was hard to contain my tears as this vision and feeling once again got the best of me. One of the couples who were there saw what was happening to me, and so after the Rosary, they brought me to the next room and asked me what was wrong. This couple was also part of our Prayer Group and they had been familiar with some of the visions I had recounted to the group during the testimony part of our prayer meetings. I explain to them what I had just received and what it meant. I honestly can't remember what they said to me that night, but I know that they did their best to try to comfort me. That next Thursday during the prayer meeting, the couple got up and recounted what I had said to them that night at the Posada. Then they disclosed that about seven hours later after the Posada, 2 family members of theirs, were killed in an automobile accident. The group was visibly stunned of what had been recounted during that testimony. I don't think they knew how to react to it because prior to me showing up the meetings, they were not accustomed to hearing the things that I was giving to say with the visions and so forth.

My next experience with feeling more than 2 deaths at a time after the Hise's, came in the middle of the night during an electrical storm. The power had gone out at my house around 3 am. or so, and someone within the house had called the power company to come fix the power outage. I had gone to the living room because I heard the power company trucks in the driveway and I saw that they were working on the utility pole about 20 or so yards in front of the house. Their trucks were being illuminated by their flashing lights and by the flashes of lightning in the dark sky. A few minutes of observing them, this disturbance hit me, but it was somewhat different than the previous ones I had received up to that point. This disturbance was death once again but it felt like a multitude of souls all at once. It was like I knew that it was more than just a few. Again, the Lord infuses this knowledge of what I am feeling, and this felt like a ton of souls that were dying all at once. It was like I felt all their pain all at once. I immediately started to pray for mercy for these souls. This pain was a little more difficult to carry than the single or double deaths that I've felt at once. As morning came, I looked online and checked out the news as I did on some mornings after breakfast and I saw on one of the news sites, that a Chinese airliner went down and 300 souls perished. I immediately did a search for the timeline of the crash and it coincided exactly to the minute that I felt the disturbance and of the pain of a multiple to souls hitting my soul at once. This seemed like another level that the Lord brought me to in seeing death.

I've been given that grace many times over now over the years, in seeing multitudes die at once. The 2 largest ones were through dreams. The largest one was the Myanmar Cyclone Nargis of 2008. Nearly 140,000 souls perished in this deadly natural disaster. In the dream, I dreamed of the Earth like one sees it from Space. I then see what seemed like a swarm of black dots or something like that going towards that region of the world. If one imagines a swarm of bees attacking something, this is what that looked like. I prayed for these souls because I knew death was coming. I even drew a picture of this scene in my journal. I viewed it as a legion of Angels of Death descending down to collect these souls. I didn't feel this one though. I don't think my soul could've handled all that pain all at once during that time of my life. Perhaps that is why the Lord God gave me the dream only and not the feeling with it.

The second largest was a Chinese Earthquake that took place in my early years, that claimed something like 3000 plus souls at once. In this dream, I dreamed exactly about the earthquake. The dream was the day before it happened. God once again, showed His Infinite Mercy towards them by allowing prayers of Mercy for their souls before they died in this terrible quake halfway around the world. Like the first dream, I didn't feel this, it was the dream only. I still mourned for all these souls just like all the rest that I had been given to pray for and like always, no one was aware of what I was given to see.

There are times when God allows me to know exactly who is going to die and is need of prayers of mercy beforehand but there are also times when He doesn't show me. He just wants me to pray on their behalf. I use to ask Him to show me whose death it was I was feeling when I wasn't shown. I came to realize later that there are just times I don't need to know that information. I just needed to trust in His Mercy and pray for their souls and that was it.

That was the case in the Summer of 2010 when one of the members of the Prayer Group, had his 4-year-old son kidnapped from his house in the middle of the night. Being from a small town, crimes such as this are such rare occurrences. This became a media storm. It came to be that a family friend of theirs, who had done some remodeling work at their house, was the main suspect. This young man was a part of the Spanish Youth Group and on occasion, visited our prayer group as well. The police brought him in and questioned him. After a few hours of interrogation, he led the police to where he had the boy sequestered. When they arrived at the abandoned house near the workplace of this young man, the little boy had passed away. It was determined that the 4-year-old boy died of heat exhaustion. It was said that he was tied up and wrapped in a blanket. The combination of the unforgiving Texas July heat and the fact that the house was abandoned and closed up, contributed to his death. This was a huge shock to us all and so heartbreaking to the little boy's family. Somehow, the young 23-year-old man escaped police custody, and a large manhunt was underway. He was tracked down a day later and was shot to death. They said he had a weapon and drew on the law enforcement officers. A lot of people, who attended the little boy's funeral, also attended the young man's funeral as well. I attended both. It was all so surreal.

I wrote in my journal the day before the kidnapping took place that I had received a disturbance and that it felt like death. This was the situation in which the Lord did not show me whose death it was. My job was just to pray for mercy, and I did. When my family and I went to go visit the grieving boy's parents at their house. The house was packed with family and friends. Everybody was there for support and offering their condolences. Even the big city news were outside looking for interviews. They approached me but I declined out of respect for the grieving family. We entered the bedroom where some close members of their family were, they were just giving support to the grieving father the best way they could. We tried to do the same. The mother wasn't there, she had been sedated because of the incredible grief she was experiencing. The dad saw me after we were in his room for about a minute and he approached me and embraced me. He was just weeping and saying to me, "why did this happen? Why? Why?" I just gave him some consoling words and I said that I would be offering my prayers for them. In the back of my mind as he was embracing me, I knew that this was what the Lord had granted me to see and feel 2 days before. Only God knows why He chose not to reveal the identity of these impending deaths in this tragic event. I trust that it was for the best.

There are also situations when the feeling of death just lingers and I pray for Mercy but the feeling just continues despite the continued prayers for the soul. In cases like this, there are 2 reasons, the first is that there are multiple deaths coming. Meaning, one after another and not all at one time. The second reason is that a person is struggling to die and are holding on to life, and are in need a lot of prayers before they pass. The second reason, is harder to deal with because it's very spiritually and mentally draining for me. It has gotten to the point many times where it's drained me so much, that it becomes necessary for me to seek help in form of support. Usually, I keep things like this close to the vest, but in those situations, I tell the Lord that I can’t handle it much longer. He usually sends me someone who helps me through these trying times. The help comes in the form of them just listening to me, and that's usually just enough support to get me through it.

In the first situation, the consecutive deaths happen more frequent than all the other ways that I'm given to see death. I call them "clusters of death".

In early 2016, we had 4 members of our parish pass away in like a 2-week span, and in those 2 weeks, the feeling of death was a constant one. Each one was given to me through a dream but with the "feeling" attached to it. It was like clockwork, the dream, and then the death the next day. It was like that pretty much for all 4 deaths. As each death occurred, I felt like my soul took a major beating and by the last death, I was absolutely spent. When these "clusters" do come, there are times when I do receive some spiritual relief in the form of a deep peace, but it's usually short-lived. I know that it will be a short break and so that makes me enjoy those moments to the max, and that gets me ready for the next soul that needs prayers of mercy.

In those 4 deaths that occurred, and with a lot of the deaths I'm given, I'm "connected" with the family of the dying person. The Lord allows me to be connected with them on an emotional level till the death occurs. The strangest feeling I get is after the death occurs. That is when that connection ends. I feel somewhat empty like there was nothing there in the first place. The sadness, the hurt, the pain, everything, is gone in an instant. The families are left to mourn and I'm on the outside with no feeling of what had just occurred. I do mourn with them in a way afterwards though. Most of them will never know of the connection I had with them. That's a little hard on me. I've wanted so many times, to tell the grieving families of God's incredible Mercy upon their loved one's souls. To tell them, what He allowed me to see and to feel before they passed. I believe that would give them some comfort in a way. That's one of the reasons I decided to write this book, to show people that God's Mercy is alive and well, and working powerfully among us all!

The second situation, in which a soul is struggling to die and are hanging on to life, is just as difficult as the first situation.

A case in the Summer of 2015 is an example of that. The feeling of death started in early July, and I kept praying and praying the Chaplet of Divine Mercy with no relief of the pain I was feeling. It started with a "cluster" in late June that was very difficult on me but had ended. Then this disturbance started soon after that, The feeling that began in the first part of July, ran into mid-July. It was beginning to take its toll on me. I am still able to perform my daily routine, while these spiritual things are happening within my soul. My mood is the only thing affected by this. I get quiet and I'm easily frustrated by the smallest things. I get irritated very fast as well. I reacted worse in the early years and I use to confess it quite often. I've gotten better in handling it by God's Grace, but as I have, the disturbances have become a lot stronger and more frequent.

Since 2009, I've been the Confirmation teacher at our parish and also I've helped out with the Youth Group and by 2015, I became the head Youth Minister. We were preparing for our Youth trip to New Orleans, when I found out the source of this major disturbance. It was less than a week before we had to take off to New Orleans, when some of the girls came in on a Wednesday night when we usually meet, and they looked very distraught. One of the older girls came to me and the new Director of Religious Education and said, that one of the girls that was part our group, had just lost her mom to cancer. This was a major shock to us because there was no indication from her or anybody else, that her mother was ill. It was right after we got this terrible news, that my mind connecting all the dots. The lingering death feelings, the disturbances, the hanging onto life, it was all this, this young girl's mother. I had just talked to the new DRE about everything I was feeling from early July to that point when we received this heartbreaking news.

I had known the DRE for about seven or so years. She knew a lot about what I was going through because she was one of the people I went to when I was struggling with all these visions and things from God. She became a very good and trusted friend of mine.

After my mind had connected all the dots with this tragic news, the realization that what I was carrying all this time, was the death of this cancer-stricken woman. Everything that I felt, left just like that and the peace returned. I did feel extremely sad for the girl, losing her mother at such a tender age. The mother was in her 30s. The daughter was only 15 and had several siblings, a couple of them very young.

Chapter 6. Death by Suicide

In the 10 years of this incredible an unforeseen journey that the Lord has me on, death by suicide has been the rarest of all the deaths that I've been given to see and pray for. There have only been 3 of them and 1 attempted one that didn't succeed.

Part of what I have received from Above, is what was described to me by my mysterious Australian friend that I wrote about earlier as, a "supernatural empathic gift". This "gift", played a central role in the all 4 cases.

This spiritual gift, some people may have experienced something like it. To be empathic for example, is like when a friend or family member is feeling sad or depressed or whatever and you "feel" it as well. It's more than sympathy, you actually take on the emotional traits of that person. This empathic "gift" can also extend out to strangers and random people, and it can strike at any time. It can very difficult to be around people at times like I described earlier, about not being able to go out in public. This gift that I received pretty quickly in my conversion, was one of the reasons for that. One can pick up so many things from so many different people. This empathic gift, like a lot of gifts, also has a dark side to it. People will often confuse or even abuse this gift. Aura readings, energy readings and New Age things like these are not of God. One can read in the "Acts of the Apostles 16:16", and see what I'm talking about. Some "gifts" can be from a demonic source. I've had enough experience with the "dark side" to know the difference what's of God and what is not. An example of this, is a story I read about somewhere on how this particular woman in the 19th century, wanted to be considered a living Saint and she made a so-called deal with the devil to receive many spiritual gifts. Gifts like the gift of healing, visions, and other extraordinary supernatural ones. She was considered to be very saintly because of these gifts. There was a price to pay for that deal, because on her deathbed, the woman had to receive an exorcism to break that so-called deal. It was quite a scary sight as the story goes, seeing the women being exorcised at that moment, as described by the priest who performed the exorcism.

At times, I will "receive" someone's feelings, emotions, pain, hurt, etc., before a particular person actually does. The reasons are to help that person carry some of the "load", and to make sure that enough prayer is offered up on their behalf. In these 4 cases, and of all the overall cases in the last 10 years, the suicide in 2016 was possibly the most impactful, and most powerful experience for me since it all began in 2006.

In the Spring of 2016, I received the "disturbance" both before, and during this death/suicide. A few days before the death, all the feelings associated with an impending death came to me, but it was a little different than most, I even made a note of it on my phone. I wrote about the loneliness and the despair that I was receiving. I also wrote, "I can "feel"(sense) someone's suicidal thoughts". It was a rough night to say the least, because it wasn't the only death I was feeling that night. Flash forward to 3 days later, and the death feeling began again and it was triggered as it sometimes is, by something I saw. In this case, it was a simple picture of a girl that I saw on social media. The feeling escalated fairly quick while I was working, to the point that I had to ask a couple of people via text to pray for me. One of the people I texted, was the girl from the picture I saw on this popular social media site. She ignored my plea, but the other person did respond and did offer their prayers. I had to stop working a few times because the feeling was beginning to overwhelm me. The negativity that came with it was very strong but I was able to pray for mercy for this person because I "knew" someone was about to die, and die very soon. It was very distinct. My thoughts were, "they will see what they did to me after I'm gone". It was like I was the one who was about to die. It felt like someone was piercing my soul with a knife and they were twisting and turning it till the pain was becoming too much for me. Then in an instant, all of it was lifted from me. I "knew" at that moment someone had just died. My "connection" ended and there was no more pain. I get a call less than an hour later and I was told about a death that had just occurred, a suicide. The body had just been found. I told the person what I had just "experienced" earlier. This was confirmation to all that was "given" to me. I know without a doubt, that God in His unfathomable Mercy, had mercy on this troubled soul who took their own life. I don't think I've fully recovered from that death. I gladly and willingly accept that experience all over again in order for a soul to receive mercy from Our Lord. God is Mercy!

To be "connected" to someone at their moment of death, especially that type of death, is something that was humbling in a way, in terms of being allowed to experience that moment. I've experienced moments of this nature before but never this personal or powerful.

I believe this empathic gift was given to me in order to be able to pray for people with more vigor, with more of a desperation factor and therefore, more effective in my prayers, but only by God's Grace. It's nothing of my doing. I also believe that a lot of what I "feel" now, is not my own anymore, at least a large majority of it, and that is rough. I've learned to control what comes in for the most part. Many people suffer more than a lot of us can imagine and I'm so grateful that God allows me to help carry some of that for them and with them. Praise be to God!

The other case worth noting was an attempted suicide in early 2015. Just after I had finished teaching on a Wednesday night to the Confirmation class, a young girl approached me right before youth group started.

In 2015, we had Catechism and youth group on the same night and so it got pretty hectic on some nights. I quickly went to go grab the then 9th-grade teacher, my trusted friend who is the Director now, and we went to one of the makeshift classrooms which doubled as a cry room for Sunday Mass. The young girl then proceeded to tell us what had occurred just the previous week. She starts by telling us that she had just gotten out of the hospital because she tried to take her life by downing a bottle of pills. Stress, school, and family problems brought it all on. It is similar to what a lot of kids go through it seems like nowadays. It just got too much for her to handle. This young girl realizing what she had just done, went to her family and told them what she had just happened. They took her to the hospital immediately where they quickly pumped her stomach. She then continued with her story as tears rolled down her face. The doctors had told her and her family that the number of pills and the length of time that the pills were in her system, that she should've died from that, and that it was a miracle that she was alive. She finished her story by recounting that while she stayed a couple of days in the hospital recovering, she witnessed some other families going through similar tragedies, attempted suicides, and suicides. It made her realize that life was precious, that her life is precious. After she had finished the story, we gave her some encouragement and we prayed for her. It was the first time for us, as teachers that we had to deal with something like this.

When I got home, I went through my phone, through my notes, and I saw that I had put down exactly what the young girl recounted to us just an hour or so earlier. I had put it down in my notes exactly the same time frame while she was going through this incredibly tough situation. The suicidal thoughts, the pain, every feeling she felt, I wrote down that I was feeling it all. I prayed with much fervor during that period as I always do when something this strong comes to me. I realized that the Lord allowed me to experience through this empathic gift, this incredible tribulation with this young girl, in order for His Divine Mercy to shine forth. The miracle that came about that the doctor told the family, was God's Divine Mercy. He gave me a front row seat to that! Thank You Lord!

The other 2 cases were not as dramatic as the first two, but their souls were just as important and God's mercy was out in full force.

These empathic "connections", in which I call them, can sometimes be so in tuned with a particular person, that it can be very taxing on me spiritually and emotionally. Throughout the 10 years of this life, the Lord has given to "connect" with certain people. It starts usually starts with me being drawn to them. It's a spiritual thing in which my soul recognizes that the "connection", is different than the average person. The person, the soul, is not any better or worse, but different. Then I usually start having dreams about them, and then typically it's something that has actually happened to them in real life, or something that will happen to them in the very near future. At this point, I've already made contact with the person and have begun somewhat of a friendship with them. This is when I usually find out that the dreams had a prophetic tone to them. I then introduce some of what God has granted me, in order for them to understand how I "knew" certain things about them. The empathic gift then becomes fully activated if you will. I then start to have these emotions, feelings, and thoughts that this person is having as well. I see it as like my soul has become infused with theirs for a certain amount of time. This becomes a very delicate time for me at this point, because I become emotionally tied to them. I become "one" with them. I do not see how it's possible to get more intimate with a person than this, becoming "one" with their souls. Being tied to them happens because the Lord has something that needs to be relayed to them, like a message or something of that nature. It's usually something that is not what the person wants to hear. On rare occasion though, it is, but not very often. Finally, the "connection" reaches a critical point when the message is given to the person. Everything has been established at that point, the friendship, their knowledge and a somewhat understanding of my "life". It's more than enough information for them to believe that what I am telling them is from God. This is the point, the juncture, that the "connection" is severed. The friendship typically ends at this point because like I said earlier, the message is something that they usually aren't prepared for and typically, it was something they didn't want to hear. I feel empty for quite a bit after the "connection" has ended. To lose that type of intimacy with another soul is never easy. To have shared in their suffering, pain, or whatever, is a grace from God. With the friendship ending, the communication has ceased and that's equally as hard on me, but I did what the Lord asked me of me. Sometimes I feel like "what's the point ", knowing that these people aren't going to listen to the message, but I still deliver it anyway.

When the first "connection" happened, it was very unique in feeling. It was an incredible and somewhat euphoric feeling. I had never experienced something like that up to that point. I just knew, had this knowledge that the person I was sitting next to, that I was infused with her soul. That "connection" happened at a Charismatic Renewal conference in Ft Worth, Texas. We were all sitting in this high school auditorium listening to some speaker talk about something that I really don't remember, because I was so entranced with this new feeling. I initially thought the reason this "connection" happened, was because God had this person in mind for me as a future relationship, potential spouse, or something like that. I ended up giving this person a message and then with that, it all ended.

These "connections" usually happen with females. Someone said to me it was because women are more spiritual than men. There was one young man that I prayed over once, probably a couple years into this life that I felt a possible "connection" but nothing was ever established.

Sometimes I wonder if its God who chooses the person I "connect" with, or if it's just part of the gift He has granted me through His Holy Spirit.

With most people, I can focus on them and just start to feel them, feel their soul, feel who they are. Again, is it part of the gift or is it God choosing who I feel? It has to be all God because nothing is done without His Will.

A couple of years or so into going to these weekly prayer meetings at the church, I would tell my mom that I would have dreams about laying hands on people and praying for them. In some of these dreams, healing would occur. At most of these prayer meetings, several of the older members of the group including my parents, would pray by laying hands on people. On this particular night, my mom called me over to help pray for this lady and I did. I laid hands on her and I prayed and that was the beginning of many people that I have laid hands on and prayed for.

Through this empathic gift, along with the gift of knowledge, and of seeing the condition of souls, the Lord has granted me to experience some incredible things while laying hand and praying for people.

I would "see" by laying hands on these people, what they were praying for. I would ask them if they were praying for a specific person or for a specific intention and they would always nod their heads yes. The Lord allowed me to tap into their souls and into their prayers. Even by just holding hands with a person, like during mass during The Our Father like we do in our parish, I could "see" many things within them. I could "see" and I would "know" their sins at times. When I explained this "gift" to a deacon once about what the Lord had granted me through this, he told me that I was sinning by intruding in people's privacy. I was taken aback by that. Sometimes it just comes to me without any effort on my part. How can that be a sin? To me it was all God's will.

As I wrote about a little earlier, I didn't even need to touch the person in order to "see" within them.

There was one occasion in late 2009, when my parents and I went with a small group from our church to this Charismatic conference/concert at an out of town church. This beautiful church was dedicated to Our Lady of Mount Carmel. Adoration had begun towards the end of this event and needless to say, it got very electric in there because of the presence of our Lord and Savior in the Holy Eucharist. I was sitting with a young friend of mine when this powerful experience began. I could not only just a "feel" all the people there, I started to hear all what the packed church were praying for. I don't know if I heard it audibly or not, but it was so clear to me to where these prayers were coming from. I began to point out to my young friend who was praying for what. There was so much pain there, so many people asking for so many different things. I could "feel" it all as well. It was so overwhelming to experience all that at once.

Sometimes I would become weary of praying with a large group, or even a small group of people because my personal prayer would get drowned out by the prayers of everyone else. This empathic gift allows me to "feel" everything but myself at times. I really have to focus in order to pray personally for myself in a group situation. As my spiritual life has grown, that has become easier for me to do. There are times though where it doesn't matter how focused I am on myself, the feelings of everyone just breaks through. Perhaps it's just the Lord just telling me in that situation, "this isn't about you Jose" and He sends me something or someone that I need to pray for.

Chapter 7. Lourdes and Paris, France 2015

In the Fall of 2015, my parents and my oldest sister and I received a beautiful grace. We went on our fourth pilgrimage overseas. We went to Spain and then to France. This was our second trip to France and our second trip to Spain.

Of the four pilgrimages, nothing compares to Lourdes, France. We've traveled all over Italy and all over Spain and Portugal as well. We visited all the holy sites in all those countries and Lourdes, France is my favorite out of all of them by far. Lourdes is perhaps the first or second most famous Marian apparition site. It's our parish namesake, Our Lady of Lourdes, The holiest part of this Pyrenees town, is the Grotto where Our Lady appeared to St Bernadette in 1858. Millions of pilgrims have traveled to this holy spot for many years. Many tears have been shed here and many prayers have been said here as well, including my own.

I believe it was our second day in Lourdes when I ventured alone to the Grotto once again to pray at the spot of the apparitions. They have benches set up in front of the Grotto where people sit and just pray or participate in the many Masses that take place throughout the day there. This was the first opportunity I had to be on my own after the scheduled tour that we had earlier that day. I had become very familiar with the layout of this beautiful small town in southern France, from our first pilgrimage in 2008. I sat in one of the back rows of the benches and I began to pray. Very quickly a flood of pain and hurt came upon me. It was so much so that I began to weep. My whole purpose of wanting to go to Lourdes once more and be at the spot of where the Queen of Heaven appeared numerous times to a poor peasant girl, was to seek answers to some pressing issues I was struggling with. I did not expect what I received at that moment. All the petitions and prayers of mercy, and desperate hope, from all the pilgrims gathered on that mid-Fall afternoon, enveloped my soul. I've never experienced that much that fast in my 10 years. This empathic feeling also came with an incredible disturbance. The pain and hurt were very strong, I had to walk away from the Grotto area. I had a baseball cap on and I just pulled the bill down to help cover my eyes and the tears that were falling non-stop. I just walked around trying to comprehend all this and trying to gather myself. My only thought as I walked around was, "all these people have no idea what I have just received, what I had just felt". Every time I approached the Grotto after that, all that pain and hurt and suffering came back. It was like that apparition spot was a carrier of so much human emotions. I prayed a Chaplet of Divine Mercy immediately for this major disturbance as I walked around hiding my tears and pain from the droves of pilgrims walking about. The next morning, we awoke to the news that a Russian plane had gone down and 224 souls perished. It was taken down by a bomb, a terrorist act. The major disturbance the day before at the Grotto, were these deaths by an act of terrorism. The Lord always confirms to me by His Holy Spirit on what I have received and on this solemn occasion, the Spirit of Lord confirmed to me that it was this tragedy. God had mercy on these 224 souls. I have no doubt on that. God is Mercy! That next night, I had a dream of death right before our pilgrimage continued on to Paris.

Lourdes is my favorite holy site to visit but Paris is my favorite city of all the places I've been blessed to visit. My first visit in 2008, was amazing. That was my first European city to visit and it definitely left its mark on me. On that first pilgrimage in 2008, we visited all the tourist attractions, The Eiffel Tower, The Louvre, and The Notre Dame Cathedral, we did it all.

On the 2015 pilgrimage, we had two separate stays in Paris. The whole tour bus was filled with excitement as we got closer to Paris. The first sight of the Eiffel Tower gave me chills. The whole group was like children seeing something so spectacular for the first time. Seeing everyone's reaction to that incredible landmark was wonderful. We did the whole city tour by bus before we went to the hotel, but as we circled around and passed by The Eiffel Tower a final time before we headed out to the rest of the city, I received something. It was another disturbance. It started as I was looking out the window and viewing the Eiffel Tower one final time. I received a vision at that moment. I see these moving images of the Eiffel Tower fall by an act of terrorism. I could see the city in a panic by this awful act. It was like I was in a trance with my eyes open, while seeing all these things unfold before me. It shook me as I snapped out of the trance. I quickly rebuked what I had just seen in the name of Jesus Christ, and I just prayed for this beautiful City of Lights as we headed to our hotel for the night. My mind was occupied with all the beautiful sites and tourist attractions as we were in Paris, but my soul was not at ease. We toured the Notre Dame Cathedral and we saw many soldiers with AK-47s or some type of assault rifles, just patrolling this world famous church. Everyone thought it was because of the terrorist attack on the Russian plane that had just happened. The final day in Paris was a free day for the group and many went shopping at the world famous Galeries Lafayette, which is an upscale department store. I walked around a little bit in the store but I was uneasy and so I went outside and took a walk around this huge block which contained the location of a beautiful opera house in the middle of Paris, the Palais Garnier. They were setting up for an outdoor show for a popular movie that was coming out and there was a lot of security all around. There were a sea of people walking all about the department store sidewalks, and around the opera house and I felt as lonely as I had in a long while. I felt like I was invisible in some ways. I was just praying as I circled the opera house and I then just stopped and sat on some steps. I just sat and listened to a street musician entertaining the small crowd that was sitting on the steps leading up to the entrance of this beautiful building. There were so many cars that were just passing through the busy city center of Paris, and I was just observing it all from my vantage point. I saw many couples walking and many tourists as well from all over the world just enjoying themselves. There were so many people with smiles on her face, just enjoying the moment and I was just there sitting on those steps with my soul wounded. A week after we got back from Paris, once again tragedy struck. I saw on the news as did the world, the horrible terrorist acts that occurred in Paris that claimed 137 lives. My immediate thought was of the vision I had received on the bus ride heading into Paris, and also of the feeling I had that last day as I sat on the steps of the opera house. The Lord had allowed me to see what was going to happen to this beautiful city. He gave me the grace, the beautiful grace, of praying for the city and the victims before this horrendous act took place. I mourned with the rest of the world but this tragedy struck me deeper than any other act of this nature that I had received. I believe it was because I was actually there shortly before it happened and because of my affinity to this city. Many people including myself, placed the French flag over our profiles on social media honoring the victim and the country and once again my thoughts, as it is in these situations, is that no one in this world knew what I was given to experience the week before this deadly attack. Once again though, I know without a doubt that God had mercy on those 137 souls.

I wanted to come back different from this last pilgrimage in 2015. I wanted to be more dedicated, more consecrated to Our Lord and to Our Lady. In some ways, I did come back different. The level of the empathic feelings, the deaths, the knowledge, went to an all time after that point. The clusters of death that I wrote about earlier, came fast and nonstop it seemed like at that point as well. There were more tragedies, terrorist acts, and deaths after that, that the Lord had granted me to see beforehand and granted me the Grace to pray for mercy at each moment before these deaths occurred.

It's not a case of me being shown these things beforehand in order for these tragedies to be prevented, it's for the grace to pray for mercy on their behalf. God grants us all free will and some men choose evil instead of good but God's infinite mercy prevails. In the end, these evildoers, these terrorists, don't have the last word, God's Mercy does. Praise be to God!

Paris became a turning point like I said. The Belgium attacks that claimed 30 plus souls, was given to me to pray after Paris and so was the San Bernardino attacks in California as well.

The night before the San Bernardino attack that claimed 14 innocent victims, I received the knowledge of the terrorist attack that was about to occur. I remember very clearly thinking that an attack, a terrorist attack was about to occur and I prayed again for mercy for these victims, for the future victims as it was at that point. I didn't ask God where this was going to occur, my job was only to pray for mercy for them, and He did show mercy on them upon their deaths.

Chapter 8. Orlando, June 2016

From Paris to Belgium to San Bernardino, the Orlando terrorist attack has been on par with them, as far as worldwide outrage and sense of loss. These acts of violence have become way too common since late 2015 and into 2016. The rate of these attacks is alarming to say the least, but God's infinite Mercy prevailed in these senseless acts of violence.

Amid the mourning and loss, I take some comfort in knowing that the Lord allowed me to pray for these numerous souls before their lives were taken, and this includes the 49 Orlando victims.

24 hours before the Orlando attacks, I woke in the middle of the night with this sense of anxiety. I've gone through some bouts of anxiety ever since I was diagnosed with diabetes in 2010, but I knew that this episode was something different. It felt like my soul and my insides were being crushed by some force. Then the anxiety made way for something evil. This evil feeling was accompanied by a feeling of death. The Lord allowed me to know that death was on the horizon and that I needed to pray for mercy for souls. I got off my bed at that moment and I got on my knees and prayed the Chaplet of Divine Mercy for the impending deaths that were about to occur. I did struggle through the Chaplet because of the feelings I was receiving were quite extreme. By the grace of God, He allowed me to go to sleep peacefully after that, for the remaining few hours I had left before I had to get up.

There was another occasion where the feelings I had, were similar to what I felt before the Orlando attacks.

During my 2010 pilgrimage to Portugal and Spain, we toured the presidential palace in Madrid, which is used ceremoniously now, and I experienced something awful there while taking the tour. I barely made it through the tour because I felt like I was being crushed on all sides, I could hardly breathe and I couldn't gather my thoughts. I had to stop multiple times. It wasn't till I walked out of the palatial grounds, that all these feelings left.

We found out through the tour guide, that many souls were executed there in the courtyard many years ago by the Spanish government. All those excruciating feelings that I felt, was the death of all those souls.

The next day after the Orlando massacre, I was still feeling the lingering effects of the night, the evil and the death feelings. I reached out to a person who helped me get through a rough stretch that had started a couple of months prior.

I recounted to this young woman, whom I met a few months earlier, what I experienced during the night.

There's a need for me to have an outlet for all these things that the Lord allows me to feel and to see and to do. This young woman named Valerie and her younger sister Yaretzi, whom I met a couple of years earlier, helped me tremendously. For them just listening to me, was just enough to get me through the current "mission", which the Lord had sent me. Their support and soothing presence, was a grace from God.

The Lord has sent me certain people at critical times on my journey, to help me cope with whatever it is He's asking of me. These 2 sisters, were a Godsend through the roughest stretch since this "life" began. I can't thank them enough.

I didn't hear about the Orlando massacre until the following morning as most people did. When I read what had occurred, the Holy Spirit confirmed to me as He usually does, that this was what I was given to pray for just the day before. The evilness, the death, the crushing of my soul, it was all this.

Many people were affected by this violent act. Outrage, pain, and sadness, rang throughout the country and beyond. My feelings dissipated pretty quick. I felt a little empty after these extreme feelings I had just gone though left. This happens on occasion, as I wrote about earlier. I feel cold and perplexed. It's like I'm completely emptied out with no trace of anything of what I had just experienced. Perhaps it was the Lord granting me relief, after that long stretch of deaths I had just gone through.

This massacre brought out a lot of strong opinions, out of a lot of people. Everything from religion, to gun control, to the people themselves who were in the club that night.

These souls from Orlando, and those countless more prior, whom the Lord allowed me to pray for before they died, were in need of prayer, in need of mercy upon their souls. That's the sole reason I was given this gift of seeing death. The large majority of us aren't spiritually ready to die, but God's infinite mercy grants souls like those in Paris, Orlando and those I've written about, mercy. There are a multitude of deaths that occur daily that perhaps don't get that same grace, probably it's because there may be nobody to pray for them. Maybe there are others like myself who have been granted the same grace of seeing death. God only knows.

I 100% believe, and follow, the teachings of the Holy Catholic Church. Many people distort or aren't fully knowledgeable on what she teaches and that causes much undue hatred towards her. God is Mercy, that I know first hand but He is also a Just God. We all must turn to God's Mercy if want to achieve peace in this world and as I write this, we are so far removed from God and peace, that it's frightening. God have mercy on us all!

When people say that someone died before their time, or that this person's life was cut short and had so much left to do, my thoughts are exactly like what my old Irish priest Father Nagle use to say over and over again. He said as soon as we are born, actually the moment of our conception, our time is counting down. I believe that each of us have a specific day that we're going to die. Seeing and receiving all these deaths, just confirms that to me each time that it happens. We all have our set number of days, and it's up to us to do what we can with those days. Do we use them to serve God or to serve the world?

Chapter 9. The Unbelievers

As with anything that one does, more so when dealing with the supernatural, there are unbelievers and naysayers. I've had my share of them of over the years and many a time, the Lord proved me right.

When I first started to receive all the gifts from above, I thought people, specifically those in the prayer group, would be so supportive and understanding on how the Lord was working through me.

I know when the testimony part of our prayer meetings would come up, no one gave testimony similar to what I was receiving. I was a little apprehensive at first because like I said, no one was speaking about the supernatural. Most of their testimonies were about certain things going their way, or a medical test result coming back good, or things of that nature. God works in all ways so I'm not belittling the blessings they received. My testimonies, were so far away from everyone else's, that I guess it was inevitable that the unbelievers and some resentment would come my way, and it most definitely did.

On one Thursday night, as we gathered at our weekly meeting place at the church hall, three brothers came as they would on occasion do the music and at times, share with the group as well. Their mother was the one whom I first laid hands on to pray.

On this night, I gave a testimony to what seemed to be common for me in those days, something of the supernatural. After I sat down, the middle brother got up and gave testimony on something that I really don't remember what it was, but he started it off by saying, "this isn't something like Jose's gifts but nonetheless it is something of God". He said in a tone like I was bragging in a way, and he was making himself appear humble by comparison. I was taken aback by that. We were there to give testimony to God, not to compare our testimonies, as he seemed to be doing.

In another instance, one of the younger girls who attended the group also made a comment on how every time I got up and gave testimony, it seemed like I was bragging and full of pride. I was surprised by that comment as well.

In both these instances and others that occurred, these people didn't fully know the struggle I was going through during those early years as I look back on it now. They didn't know of my scrupulosity. They didn't know about my many confessions of what I thought was spiritual pride. They didn't fully know my background prior to showing up to those meetings. They didn't know that my standing there, was a miracle of Divine Mercy. They were not looking at me with their eyes of their souls. There were some that did though, but those that didn't, they were the main reason the group did not last beyond my fourth year there. The group after my fourth year had turned into a self-purpose, self-fulfilling group. The Lord broke that group up because it ceased to be of Him anymore.

One of those unbelievers, was key in this prayer group breaking up. From late 2008 to early 2010, was a period of me receiving messages from God, in order for me to pass it along to most everyone in the group. There were many occasions where these messages were truly confirmed about being from God. After many testimonies to that fact, this unbeliever wasn't convinced when it came down to their message from God.

This person, a young woman in her mid 20's, was one of my strongest "connections" in my 10 years. She was given many things in the forms of "proof" from Above to make her believe, but for some reason she didn't.

I believe this young woman, was very unsure of herself and she was very sheltered to a point. There were some things that she was involved with, that I'm sure that her family would not approve of. She was living a double life so to speak. Being somewhat sheltered probably led to that.

I was given a very powerful message for her, a message of repentance and a message of impending death among her family.

5 times, I was given to tell her that death was coming, and 5 times death occurred. It was after the fourth time that the message was given, that the family finally complained to the Deacon and to the young priest at the time who was there at the start of my conversion. The mother of this woman had already complained about me to the young priest prior to this, but nothing came from that.

This time, the fourth time, something did happen. I received a phone call while I was at work from the Deacon, saying that he and the young priest wanted to meet with me the next day in the church office. The Deacon didn't want to say what it was about, all he said was that they wanted to talk to me. I had already been given to know, unbeknownst to him, that this was going to happen, that this meeting was going to take place, and what it was going to be about from the Lord.

I arrived at the church office on a Friday morning and I patiently waited to be called into this old and small office. The priest and the Deacon, both gave me a cordial greeting before they started in on the main issue. As the young priest began, the very first thing he said really upset me. He pretty much had made up his mind about me, meaning he had already taken the side of this young woman.

He said to me, "first of all, we are not going to remove you from teaching the Confirmation class since you're doing it on a volunteer basis". I was stunned. Why did he open up with that? Why was that even an issue about removing me? I later came to find out that the Deacon had gone around asking about me, asking the then DRE about my competence, asking about my "experiences".

The Deacon had been part of the prayer group way before I was there, and by the time I started attending, he was just an occasional visitor. He did have some knowledge of what I had been given by God up to a certain point. He would often at times comment to me that his testimony and "experiences", were similar to mine, which wasn't true in my view. He had no clue to who I was before I was a part of the group, or even when I was in the group either.

The young priest to his defense did somewhat leave some room, albeit small room, to possibly believe that this situation could've been misconstrued.

After the priest finished telling me what he had to say, I did something that I have a real disdain for, I had to defend myself. I was fully aware of reading about the lives of the Saints, that even though they were accused of certain untrue things, they kept silent and just took the misleading claims against them. I knew I had to defend myself, I knew that the priest and the Deacon had to know what God was giving me, was in fact not just for me, but for the good of this young woman. I told them when the Lord allows me to know that there is an impending death, it's going to happen.

The priest then said to me, "death happens all the time, I could say my neighbor is going to die and eventually in two or three years, he dies. That does not mean that it was a prophetic message". I then replied, "it's not like that, its going to happen, and happen soon". He just gave me a look like he didn't believe me. The only thing that came about from this meeting was that I was not to have any contact with this woman for a while because she was traumatized according to the Deacon. I left the priest's office very upset. I felt betrayed by this woman and her family. I thought, "how could they sit with me and pray with me during all this time, and still betray me in this way? Why didn't they just come to me and try to and talk it out?" These thoughts kept running through my head over and over again.

I passed along what had happened to my father and my mother, and they were just as upset as I was. My father talked to the young priest the next day, and let him know that the group that was started some 25 years earlier, was coming to an end.

This wasn't the same prayer group when I first started attending just 4 years earlier. The group that gave me so much in terms of allowing my spiritual growth to move along at the Lord's pace. This group now, was just a shell of its former self at that point.

Two weeks later, my mother comes to me straight after the Spanish mass on Sunday and tells me that the family of the young woman, got up during the announcements, and pleaded to the parishioners for donations for a funeral, because a member of their family had just died. My mom gave me this look like even though it was a tragic death, the Lord had vindicated me.

I fully trusted in the Lord on what He had shown me with this death and I felt sadness for the family because they didn't believe. It wasn't the first time something like that had happened, and it probably won't be the last.

The unbelieving of the family, and the Deacon, and most importantly the young priest, made me want to withdraw from everything. I didn't want to attend daily mass like I had been, because I didn't want to have anything to do with the young priest anymore. How could I trust a priest who didn't believe me, who didn't support me? I even wanted to stop teaching Confirmation because I felt so betrayed. I thank God for my mother because she convinced me, not to abandon the path the Lord had put me on. Teaching and attending daily mass, were a huge part of that path.

Within two months of this, the young priest was moved to a new parish. I will admit, I felt so relieved that he was moved to another city.

All that took place in 2010, which was a very difficult year. The diabetes diagnosis, the blowup with this woman and her family and the end prayer group, all took a toll on me.

On top of all that, I was still receiving things from God but not at the pace of the previous 4 years. The diabetes played a big part in that. The diabetes that year and early the next year, clouded everything. The steady decline of my health was definitely the root of that.

The other major disbelief that came my way, had to do with my relationship with Blessed Virgin Mary. The details of Our Lady and her role in my journey, is a huge and powerful story all its own.

There were some members of the prayer group, who gathered on their own outside our weekly meetings, to discuss whether what I was testifying to about Our Lady, was indeed worthy of belief.

There were members of the group who flat out told me to my face, that they didn't believe. It was like, "why you?". I guess they couldn't believe that God could be working through one of us in the group. Especially through someone like me I guess. Once again, they were seeing me through their worldly eyes.

All this was upsetting to me. It was more upsetting that they doubted that God was working among us in this way. Their lack of faith was disheartening. I believe we lost out on a tremendous amount of graces from Our Lady because of their disbelief. I wholeheartedly believe that.

When I began with this group in 2006, this group was something special, it was of God. By mid-2010, at the end, this group was not of God anymore. This group was doing me more damage, more harm, than good. God put an end to it. The group's belief in the supernatural was blinded by their self-centeredness and their selfishness.

They tried to restart the group a few months later without my parents and myself, but it didn't last. It wasn't what the Lord wanted. I still pray for every member by name all these years later at least once a week, even with what transpired at the end with a lot of them.

There will always be detractors and unbelievers on this journey. Something that Saint Bernadette, the peasant girl from Lourdes, said that I have adopted as my belief as well, she said, "my job is to inform, not to convince". Amen!

Chapter 10. Saints, Angels, and Demons

Through this life, the Lord has granted me a peek into Heaven in a way through the many visions of His Saints and of His Angels but also, a glimpse of Hell with my many encounters with demons.

I will start with the evil first since the first part of my journey was dominated with many encounters with the demonic.

The presence of evil has its own unique feel. I've been asked more than once to describe the feeling. This is what I tell them. It has the feel, as many people will say they feel, when they believe they feel evil or some dark presence. The chills, goosebumps, the hairs on the back of their necks standing up and so forth, there's some truth to all that. It also goes deeper than that for me. I feel their presence as though they are passing through me or as if I was given to feel their essence of what they are made of. It somewhat feels a little like what I'm given to when I feel a human soul, but a soul in an incredible deep darkness. In all my research, specifically in reading about exorcisms and of the priests who've performed the Rite of Exorcism, I learned that these demonic presences, had kept the same hierarchy as they had, when they were Angels of God before they rebelled.

There are 9 Choirs of Angels and so I gather that there are 9 levels of demons as well. Through my 10 years of experience with them, that seems to be the case.

Through the grace of God and His Spirit, I can tell when it's a lower level demon compared to a higher level one. The way I feel interiorly, is the way I can tell. It feels like my soul has been dirtied, and it feels like all my insides, have been exposed to something that was rotting. The worse I feel "dirtied", the higher the level of the demon, which is accompanied by the usual other exterior signs but with a higher grade. It's a disgusting type of feeling.

Since the beginning, these dark presences have appeared as many times in my prayers with my eyes closed, as with my eyes open and not in prayer. They have appeared as dark shadows, dark blurs, and as dark, full-sized human figures. They have also taken on the appearance of Heavenly Angels as their disguise. They have also appeared with no form or shape whatsoever, but I could still feel and sense their presence. They have tried many a time, to try and hide themselves from me, but by God's grace they were exposed each time.

I did my research as I said earlier, because I wanted to understand every aspect of what I was experiencing. It gave me comfort, as I read the lives of the Saints, knowing that my experiences with the dark side, was not unique just to me. The battles that some of the Saints fought against the Evil One and his demons, were truly heroic and brave and inspiring.

To some demons, it seemed like I was their magnet. Because in the beginning wherever I went, I came away with them attached to me and it made my life very difficult. I remember having to prayed over by my parents on multiple occasions, to be rid of them.

Then after that rough period, I began to seek them out everywhere I went to see if I could feel them. If I felt them, I would then rebuke them and drive them away by the Grace of God.

During my scrupulosity period, I was so relieved that I could feel the darkness because that meant that the Lord hadn't abandoned me. Sensing or feeling anything supernatural, was my sign that He was still with me and the darkness, the evilness, was good enough for me to know that He was there. That eased my mind so many times in those early years, as strange as that sounds. I was afraid to lose all these gifts early on as well. Feeling that darkness, evilness, was also my sign that He hadn't taken these gifts away from me.

That was a huge fear that I had. I guess these gifts in those days, made me feel that I had a purpose in life, that I wasn't just a soul just passing through time without cause. I know now, that I was granted all these gifts to serve God and my fellow man.

One of the early cases of the demonic, came a couple of years after my conversion. It was well known at that point, within the prayer group, about my gift from God to be able to sense demonic presences.

My father and I were called by a lady from our prayer group, to go to one of her family member's house, where they were experiencing some disturbances. My father had many years of experience in dealing with things like this, and he was very powerful in his vocal prayer and that what was also needed in this case. He does not have the gift of sensing and feeling these spirits and so the combination of him and me, was what was called upon by God in this particular case.

We arrived at the house of this couple who was having the disturbances, on a Tuesday night after work. The couple had been complaining of something dark within their house and that something, was also keeping their children up at night. The family also claimed that they would all hear all sorts of noises in the middle of the night.

This "thing", was also causing problems between the husband and wife as well. All these signs, are typical in a demonic disturbance in a home.

My father and I walked into their home and we were greeted very graciously. We then were asked to go downstairs to where the kitchen/dining room was.

I've been to many houses throughout my life, through the carpet cleaning service that my family owns, and the layout of this house was unique to me.

We then walk down the narrow stairwell down to the dining room part of the room, and immediately the whole scene was like déjà vu. It became very surreal at that point.

This whole scene was exactly like my dream I had two days earlier. I wrote the details down exactly how their dining room was laid out. The table was exactly the same in color, and in length and in the type of wood it was made out of. The rest of the room was exactly the same as in my dream, even down to the China cabinets, and the pictures on the walls. I purposely sat down in the same seat that I had sat in during my dream, which was at the end of the table with my back towards the kitchen. It was very eerie but fascinating to me. The only difference between the dream and what was happening in real life, was who was sitting around the table. In the dream, the demon was sitting to my left and some strange creatures were taking up the rest of the seats all around the table. In real life, my father sat to my right and the wife to my left and the husband, at the other end of the table.

The husband then began to explain the disturbances. He talked about how he went downstairs and thought he was talking to his wife as he thought he saw her, but it wasn't his wife. He said it was a lady dressed in a white floor length sort of nightgown and she had black hair. She then turned around and looked at him, and then she disappeared. He got very frightened at that he said. The second instance he recounted to us, was that he went upstairs to where the master bedroom was in this unique house of theirs, and saw the same woman, just brushing her hair at the vanity table. She was taking long and slow strokes he said.

He said to us, that he wasn't really a believer in these so-called ghosts or whatever these things were, but yet he still couldn't fully explain what it was that he saw. It was at that point, as he was still talking, that I begin to feel the demonic presence. This demon was of the higher hierarchy. I could tell because I began to cringe at the strength of this fallen angel. All the typical signs of the demonic being in the house hit me all at once. This presence was very strong indeed.

I interrupted the husband, as he was about to continue on with the story, and I told everyone there that the presence had made itself known to me. The wife at that moment became visibly shaken. My father and I then proceeded to start blessing the house with Holy Water, and we started to pray this strong evil presence away. It was at that moment that the wife began to cry, and the husband made the comment to us, that the hairs on the back of his neck began to rise because he was beginning to feel this evil presence as well. We went around to the all the bedrooms, the living room and so forth, invoking Saint Michael, Saint Rafael, and Saint Gabriel the Arch-Angels, and all the Angels in Heaven, to protect the family and their house, and to drive away all these demons that were causing so much damage there. The prayers and the sprinkling of the Holy Water throughout the house lasted about 15 to 20 minutes or so. I kept praying until this evil presence that I felt so strongly, was gone.

The house was "clean". I told the frightened couple that the house was free of this demonic presence that was plaguing them. My father then proceeded to give them advice on how to make sure these demons, didn't return with more of them in the suit. He told them that they needed to start going to Mass, and to continue invoking the Holy Angels on a regular basis and to make a concerted effort to amend their lives. They agreed that change was needed and said they would do what was prescribed to them. I gave the wife a holy card of Saint Michael and told her to make sure she prayed every day. We then finished up with a little bit of prayer with this couple, and then we went on our way. They were very grateful for us helping them out. The dream I had of this house and it coming to pass, was proof to me that what my father and I did there, was God's Will.

We checked in on this couple in the following days and weeks through the family member who sent us there, to see how they were doing. We got positive reports each time. There were no more disturbances and no more fighting between the couple, everything was good. I know that I felt very good about that, knowing that the Lord sent us to do a job, and we accomplished it.

About two or three months later, we got the news that the couple ended up separating and moving out of the house, and eventually divorcing. They stopped their initial change of going to mass, and praying and so forth. In other words, they did follow through with what they were advised to do, and eventually those demons returned and this time, broke that family up.

We see the husband every once in a while and every time I see him, I think back to that night. One can only do so much with people, eventually it's up to them to follow through with whatever advice was given to them. God have mercy on them!

There was another case in early 2015 that was similar to the one I just recounted. This case had a demon plaguing the family just as bad, but that case ended with a different outcome.

The location was Ft Worth, Texas, and the people we were called to pray for, was a young single mother and her 10-year-old daughter. We were sent by a woman who is the daughter of a long-time friend of the family.

This young mother was a co-worker of the woman who sent us.

My father and I, arrived on a very cloudy Saturday afternoon to this modest three bedroom house, ready to do God's work once again.

It had been just a week since my dad and I went to another house, and prayed for a family that was experiencing a disturbance. That case was a mild disturbance, involving one of the typical weaker demons that I tend to encounter on a regular basis. We prayed for the family and the house, and the presence was gone by the power of Christ. It was a pretty easy case compared to what we were about to encounter.

Prior to that small case, we had gone through a long stretch of not doing this type of work.

The first thing we do when we encounter cases like this and others, is we ask if they have contacted a priest to come and pray for them and bless the house. In most of the cases that we have been on, they had not. They typically have an apprehension in doing that. Perhaps, it's because they fear of being considered crazy or delusional or perhaps they aren't comfortable in dealing with a priest.

We know the power that is given to the priest by our Lord in situations like this. For full on demonic possessions, a priest needs to receive permission from their bishop in order to perform an exorcism. Whatever Catholic Diocese the case falls under, they usually have an exorcist/priest within their diocese, to deal with these extreme cases of possession. Any priest can do prayers of deliverance and bless houses as part of their priestly duties. Lay people such as my father and myself, can also do the prayers of deliverance and do the sprinkling of Holy Water blessing the house. Christ Himself gave us all the power to drive out demons as He tells us in Holy Scriptures.

We started the process with this young mother and her daughter as we usually do, by getting the story of what was happening. We do this to make sure that it isn't something of the natural world that can be explained. The young mother begins to tell us about the hearing of noises. The typical doors shutting in the middle of the night, the unexplained knocks and creaks and so forth.

The unusual thing about this case was that the mother was claiming that the daughter, the 10-year-old little girl, would speak in a deep voice with an unrecognizable dialect. It frightened her. She believed that her daughter was somehow possessed.

We then began the set up of praying for them. We lit some votive candles, and I also brought with me a relic of Saint Gemma whose relics and powerful intercession, has been used by exorcists in the battling of demons. With the environment set, we were ready.

We then began to pray, as we held hands in a small circle. My father, being the strong vocal prayer force as he is, led per usual. The little girl was on my right as we held hands, and the mother, to my left.

Within minutes, this dark presence made itself known to me. As I stated before, it was a strong one. This one was so strong, that it made me cringe with quite a force. It had been a while since I'd felt something that dark. My father recognized how I was reacting, and so he asked me what it was I was seeing. I told him along with the mother and daughter, that the demon was there with us, among us. It was right behind me to my left, on the side of the mother. It wasn't until a little bit later, that we realized why it was close to the mother.

It was like I could feel the breath of this demonic presence that was standing so very close to me. I could feel it's height and stature, as this evilness gazed upon us. At that point, my father and I went around with the Holy Water, invoking the Holy Angels and invoking the Holy name of Jesus Christ, to drive away this evilness that was there and all around this house. After about 15 minutes of this, the evilness was gone.

The thing about feeling demonic presences such as this, is that it's filthiness lingers with me for a while and in this case, it surely did as well.

After talking with the mother and daughter for a bit after that, the mother finally revealed to us that she was hooked on drugs. This was the reason that the demonic presence was on her side during our little prayer circle.

There were evil spirits all around us as we were praying, and the evil spirit of drug addiction was definitely with her. That was the one that made me cringe.

Having the mother admit this drug use, was the first step of healing for her and her daughter. We gave them the usual advice that we give all the cases like this, the attending of Mass, frequenting the Holy Sacraments and so forth. We wrapped up, and the mother thanked us with such a heartfelt gratitude. Praise be to God! What a grace!

A couple of weeks after that, we got news from the friend who referred us to her, that the mother and daughter, were doing very well. The mother had enrolled her young daughter into catechism classes for the first time ever, and she and her daughter began to attend mass again on a regular basis. The mother even attended a spiritual retreat later that Fall. Glory be to God!

There was a case in 2013 that we encountered, that showed us the power of the priesthood.

This case involved a woman in her 60's who had been battling some depression and anxiety for a while, but also had her battles with the demonic. She had been prone to loud vocal outbursts, such as crying and yelling from time to time when something would trigger it. Some people could say it was because of her illness, but some of those outburst though, I believe it was demonic. How do I know? The gift of Discernment of Spirits.

This gift of the Holy Spirit, allows me to know what is of God and what is not and if it's natural or supernatural as well. In this woman's case, in this particular instance, it was of a supernatural origin.

My father and I were called again to pray for this woman. We had known this woman very well, and I had on many occasions, prayed over her. The Lord God had allowed me to "see" many things when I laid hands and prayed for her. I could "see", what she would see in her mind. I could feel her fear as well. I could "see" the darkness that she was enveloped in. I would "see" her as she was, but with this darkness. This pitch-black darkness was all around her and she couldn't find her way out. I could "see" her and her way out, the light so to speak. I would pray and talk her through this, and I would guide her to that light, and on every occasion, she "got out". This took a toll on her every time. It was fascinating to be in her mind's eye, seeing all this as she did, but from a different perspective.

In this instance though, my father and I were ineffective as we prayed over her with great fervor. We called our parish priest Father B, and he immediately came over. When he arrived at the house of this woman, that sat just outside our small town city limits, we gave him a quick rundown of what was transpiring. Our priest brought with him a small carrying case that contained a small crucifix, a small bottle of Holy Water, and some other small articles that I can't recall. It was his traveling priest kit. He entered the woman's bedroom and he quickly went to the woman's side who at this point, was very restless and hard to control as me and my father tried to hold her down. The whole scene prior to the priest's arrival looked like a scene from a movie. Hollywood often portrays scenes of exorcisms taking place with the victim, violently moving around in their bed and screaming with yells of an unrecognizable language. This real life scene was just like that.

Our priest calmly placed his small crucifix in the hand of this women, and he gently prayed for her near her right ear. Within minutes, the woman suddenly calmed down and stopped withering about. Whatever darkness she was experiencing, was gone.

While Father B was gently praying for her, I felt the darkness leave her as it passed through me. The woman then fell asleep after this great ordeal. I was amazed at the power given to him by Christ, through the priesthood. We thanked him, and as he was leaving, I tried to convey to him what I had felt throughout the whole process but with some slight apprehension. I didn't want to make the whole deal about me and so I didn't fully disclose everything that went on "beyond" his view of things.

I've had a ton more of these demon encounters, but these few cases are enough to give you an idea of what this part of my journey is like. I do wish that more of my ministry, dealt with cases like these because there's such a great need of prayers of deliverance in my town, and for exorcisms as well.

There is an old famous landmark here in my town, called The Baker Hotel. Many paranormal enthusiasts have come to my town because of this old abandoned hotel. The Baker was at one time, a nationwide tourist attraction. Many famous people, like Clark Gable, Judy Garland, Will Rogers and the Three Stooges, stayed at the "Grand old Lady", as some people call the Baker now.

My hometown of Mineral Wells was well known many years ago as having this therapeutic miraculous healing water, which was called, and is still called, "Crazy Water". Many people came in early 20th century to drink and bathe in this Crazy Water. With the military base that I wrote about earlier and this Crazy Water, Mineral Wells thrived for many years.

Once the military base was closed down, and the novelty of this Crazy Water died down, The Baker eventually closed its doors in the 1970's.

Many stories of paranormal activity began to spread throughout my small town with stories of deaths of mistresses and other types of strange deaths that took place back in the Baker's heyday. These so-called "spirits", began to "haunt" the hotel. Alleged sightings of these "spirits" began to circulate and it got the attention of paranormal enthusiasts from all over the country. There are other nearby spots that many people claim to be haunted as well with similar stories of sightings and such.

These enthusiasts, do not know what they're dealing with. These so-called "ghosts", "spirits ", or whatever, are actually demons. My extensive research and my extensive personal experiences on things of this nature, tell me so. The chief exorcist for the Vatican of over 30 years, Father Gabriele Amorth, through his many years of experience and writings, tells us the same thing.

The over enthused and curious, are actually doing a lot of harm to themselves and to our town by participating in these paranormal investigations and "ghost "walks. Most of them, if not all, just see this as something fun and interesting but in reality, it's something beyond their realm of understanding. They are bringing dark influences into their lives, and into the lives of their families and that, is potentially deadly for their souls.

The Evil One will find any way and any means to enter one's life and this "paranormal" stuff, is an easy way for him to do that.

My small town is getting more known for its bad drug problem now, more than it glorious past. I believe this infestation of drugs, is linked to all the evilness that has been brought in by these "paranormal" curiosities. I have felt the evilness all around my town.

I believe change will come though, a change for the better. Our prayers, the prayers of the faithful, for our small town are not in vain. The Lord and Our Lady will help us. I truly believe that.

The Angels made their presence known to me fairly early in my conversion. They were a welcomed relief to what seemed to be an onslaught of demonic presences.

The presence of angels in my life started in my teens. My mother told me the following story.

When I was in my mid-teens, I had gotten very ill and was confined to my bed. My room at the time, at our old house where I spent my teen years in, was converted from a two-car garage. I use to share this room with one of my brothers before he went off to college. There was a small area between my room and the original back wall of the garage in which the laundry room was situated. The small area and my room could be accessed from the kitchen/breakfast room. My mom recalls that the door from the kitchen that leads into the laundry room was slightly opened. That door had the tendency of staying open because it wouldn't stay shut. My mom says that she noticed something or someone in the laundry room, and when she looked to see who it was, or what it was, she saw an angel. The angel appeared as one would imagine it, with it's long flowing robe and with wings. She described the angel with about shoulder length hair and with a part on one side. The angel was about to enter my room she said, when it looked back at her and made brief eye contact. The angel then continued on into my room. My mother said that she froze at the sight of the angel because it caught her off guard. My mother said that the next morning, I woke up from this severe illness completely better. My mother believes that the angel was sent to heal me. Even though I have no recollection of any of it, I believe this story 100%, especially now with all the dealings I've had with the angels over the last 10 years. The only questions I have about my mom's story are, why was the angel sent in the first place and why can't I remember it. My mother's theory about the whole deal is that I was so sick, dangerously sick, that the Lord had to send an angel to heal me because of what God had in store for me in the future, namely praying for a multitude of souls.

My first encounter with the angels, after my conversion, was in a dream.

In the dream, I was sitting at the head of a very long table. A table similar to one that you would find in a school cafeteria. It was narrow, and on both sides sitting facing each other, were angels. They took on the appearance of small children, like 5-year-olds. The angels on the left had a blue color tint to them and the angels to my right had a red tint to them. The colored tint, covered everything like their heads, skin, clothes, their entire bodies. In my mind, I perceived the blue children to be the angels and the red ones, demons. The demons would blow upon the angels with their breath, and would freeze the angels in solid ice. Some unseen force would then thaw out the angels. This took place about 3 more times as I looked on. By the 4th time it occurred, I was the one thawing out the angles by my breath. This happened 2 or 3 times in succession. A full sized demon then emerged from the small ones and it took on the appearance of an elderly woman with ragged clothes. She had gray hair that was not brushed and all a mess. She frantically moved about before she took on another form.

This time, the demon took on the form of a Hispanic man in his late 40s dressed in some olive green colored pants, and matching olive green button up shirt. The demon looked like a maintenance man or a janitor. The man now multiplied himself numerous times. They all came walking out of two doorways past me. All this, was the demon's attempt to hide from me. I quickly grabbed my St Benedict medal, and my instinct was to try to uncover the demon by pressing this Holy Medal on the men as they streamed by me. My reasoning for this, was that the demon would react to the holy item pressed on him. I went back and forth, touching each man with the medal till finally, after countless men rushed by, the demon reacted with a loud whelp. The demon, retook the form of the elderly woman, and once again began to move about frantically. The scene now was in a large atrium with vaulted ceilings. These large muscular men who looked like giants, began to take apart the frame of the wall on the opposite side where the demon and I were. With their calculated movements, these giants made a large cross on the wall. One of the Hispanic men, who was one of many who multiplied, was still there. He slowly made his way to the cross. As the man got closer, he transformed into the Crucified Christ. Scourges covered His body and blood trickled down from His crown of thorns as He climbed up upon the Cross. I pointed out this moving scene to the demon and I said, "see, He died for our sins" and with that, the demon disappeared. I woke up with a profound sense that what I had just experienced, was something supernatural and profound.

From that point, my experiences with angels, increased dramatically. The next experiences came via the prayer group.

During one of our typical weekly gatherings in late 2006, while invoking the Holy Spirit as we did in the middle of our 2-hour meetings, the Lord allowed me to see my Guardian Angel. I saw my Angel with his wings covering me, as he stood behind me slightly elevated. He looked like an angel that one typically sees in pictures throughout one's life, like in books, paintings, and in churches. His robe was long and off white in color, his wings were similar in color, but with a hint of gray in them as well. He had the features of a young man no more than 20 years old, with dirty, blondish, shoulder length hair. I believe God presented my Angel to me in this way, to show me a form that I had long associated with being an angel. I stood there in awe as my Angel was protecting me from something, and was showing me that he was always with me, and always protecting me. His presence made me less fearful of the demons, and he made me feel more confident as well.

That was the beginning of my supernatural relationship, with my Guardian Angel.

There were many more occasions during my time in the prayer group, where my Guardian Angel appeared to me in the same way. My devotion to him grew even stronger because of these appearances. There was one occasion, where he appeared to me in our Church while I was praying, and he communicated with me.

In my early years, I went to the Church and prayed before Jesus ever present in the tabernacle many times. The Church became my refuge. Many tears were shed there. I was often alone during my many visits, and that allowed me to pray with great fervor, and without interruptions. I was given many graces there. Many times, I was given to feel and see the presence of angels during my fervent prayer. I would invoke their presence and asked them to join me, as I gave glory and praise to the Lord Jesus Christ. These were awesome and unforgettable moments for me, as I was among the angels surrounding the altar, and joining them in a chorus of, "Glory! Glory! Glory! To You Lord Jesus Christ!". This was truly a small taste of Heaven that I was blessed to experience.

In this particular trip to the Church, to the Chapel, as we call it now since we had a bigger Church built alongside it, I felt a presence approach me. I could tell that this presence was of a Heavenly origin. I always say when these presences approach me, that if it was not from God, for them to leave me be. That was my way of knowing what was from God or not from God, aside from the gift of Discernment of Spirits. When this Heavenly presence stayed with me, after I knew it was from Above, I asked, "who are you?", I then heard a voice say, "I'm the angel that was sent to protect you."

I then replied, "you're my Guardian Angel?", to which he replied, "yes". This was different from the other times that I was given to see my Angel in vision, because this time, I couldn't see him. I was only able to hear him and feel him.

This voice, was what I later discovered to be, an interior locution. I received many more of these interior locutions later on, from many more Heavenly visitors, but also from the demonic side.

I told my Angel, "if this is really you, I want proof". I thought to myself, "Why did I start receiving these interior voices?" Perhaps, it was just a spiritual progression that the Lord had granted me, I'm not really sure of the reasoning.

I got home and I directly went to my computer and started browsing online. It was probably within a couple of minutes or so of browsing, that I went to an early social media website. There was some music that was playing in the background on this particular page, and in those days, a small media player was attached to this page. The player showed the name of the artist and the name of the song playing, As I scrolled down to this media player, I was stunned to see what it read. The musical artists were called, "The Guardian Angels"! I believe, the album was called "The Guardian Angels" as well. I received my proof! I received my sign! My heart rejoiced knowing that what I heard, wasn't from my mind or made up, but it was truly from Heaven! It really was my Guardian Angel! Thanks be to God!

I was then granted to see many people's Guardian Angels as well from that point on. Other people's

Guardian Angels, began to appear to me at the prayer group meetings.

I've seen them individually, and I've seen them in groups. One of the most awesome sightings of these Angels, happened during the prayer meeting.

Per usual, while invoking the Holy Spirit, I saw the entire group's Guardian Angels standing right behind each one of them, as we were calling down the Spirit of God upon us. They appeared in the same form as I saw my Angel for the first time. It was an incredible sight to say the least. When I gave testimony to this after that vision, I could see on the group's faces that some believed and some didn't. Some of them, didn't know how to process it based on the perplexed look on their faces.

That awesome vision, reminded me of another vision I had during the prayer group in the early years. In that vision, I was granted to see the souls of everyone there. I was given to see who was in a State of Grace, meaning free from grave sin in their present state of life, and who was not. In the vision, I saw a lighted cross within the people who were in a State of Grace, and the ones who were out of grace, their souls were all black. That vision was a little overwhelming at the time. To be given that grace of seeing souls in that state, was incredible to me. I had been given to feel the conditions of people souls before that point, but this was an upgrade so to speak. After that night, the grace to see souls in that way continued. Sometimes, I will just look at someone for a bit, and the Holy Spirit allows me to see their souls. A priest once told me after I told him what I had experiencing in seeing souls, that I had received the gift of the Reading of Souls.

Seeing everyone's Guardian Angel from the group, was a very welcomed vision for me after that powerful vision of seeing those soul's conditions, particularly the ones whose souls were black and not in a State of Grace.

Saint Michael is the angel, along with my Guardian Angel, whom I invoke the most. Many Catholics know the image that often portrays St Michael. It is where he is standing atop of Satan, with his foot on the Satan's head as the Evil One is on the ground. St Michael, is dressed in his armored breastplate, and has his sword in hand, and is getting ready to strike Satan.

Many Catholics like myself, learned the prayer of St Michael in our youth. The prayer invokes his protection from evilness and the devil.

As my prayer life increased, the demonic experiences did as well. My prayers to St. Michael, became a multiple recited prayer throughout my day for protection from that evil.

I've had a couple of powerful experiences in regards to St. Michael. They both were in a dream and in one of them, it ended with an apparition of the Holy Arch-Angel!

In the first experience, the dream took place in my old house that I spent my teen years in. It's the same house where I had my first experience with an angel that I wrote about earlier. The dream, was a combination of a dream and a bit of the phenomenon referred to as sleep paralysis. I was sleeping in my old room in the dream, when I noticed some light coming in from the space between the top of the window and the top of the curtain. It was enough light, that it projected across the ceiling towards the door of my bedroom on the other side. The typical feeling of evil, started as I lay there in bed. From the projected light across the ceiling, I saw a countless number of evil spirits, shown as small, black jagged shapes, pass through this light as shadows. It was as though they were passing over my house, over the roof, in the area where my bedroom was. It was at that point that fear seized me, as it had in my very early encounters with demons. I then started invoking St. Michael to help me. The force of the demons had me pinned down but I was still able to speak and pray. In sleep paralysis, the person isn't able to speak and so this is where it differs from that. I fully expected to see St. Michael show up and drive these demons away. He did show, but I couldn't see him. The reason I knew he showed up, is because all the demons that were shown across the light, were gone. I was elated he came to my rescue. I woke up a little after that dream, and the terrible feeling that usually lingers when encountering demons, was still with me for quite a while as the morning went on.

The 2nd experience, is the one that made a tremendous impact on me. I've had many encounters with demons in my dreams and in most of them, I'm able to battle and pray them away, albeit with a great struggle.

This dream began a little bit before I walked into my bedroom. The demon appeared before me in a form of black smoke. I could feel its presence very strongly. Once again, fear seized me. I then quickly reached for my Holy Oil that I kept on top of my dresser, to try to throw it on the demon and drive it away. I grabbed the small plastic bottle containing the Holy Oil and I tried to open it, but to my surprise, the demon had removed the opening of the bottle. It had become just a fully enclosed small bottle with no openings whatsoever. My thought was, "that's a good one!", in reference to the demon's slick move with the bottle. Prior to my entering the bedroom, I had encountered a large scorpion while searching for one of my nephews. I assumed that the scorpion was the demon before its change to the dark smoke. I then tried to leave my room in order to escape the demon, but this evil spirit removed the doorknob as well. I was trapped. The next part, is where I'm not sure if I was awake or still dreaming, It was almost immediately, from the point when I realized that I was trapped, to the next moment where I was laying there on my bed. I then look up, as my room is now quiet, and I see St. Michael standing right next to my bed. He was facing in towards me, as he was standing by the side of my bed. He was looking straight ahead like he was on guard duty.

I could see every little detail of him from the vantage point of my bed. The first thing I noticed, were his legs. St. Michael had on sandals typical of what soldiers wore in Roman times. The leather straps criss-crossed all the way up to his mid calf. I could see the hairs on his legs, they were of a darkish blonde color and very thick. I then saw the details of his outfit. He had on a silver colored breastplate that went over his Crimson colored garment he wore underneath. His outfit was exactly like those in the many images and statues of him, a skirt type style of attire. My gaze made its way up to his stoic face. His face and his jaw line were that of a

Hollywood leading man, square-jawed and chiseled. His hair was dirty blonde and shoulder length, and a bit wavy. His eye color was the only thing I do not remember. Perhaps, it was because his gaze was stone cold like he was on duty. His muscular left arm, held a long metal rod that stood on the ground and reached the top of his head. I was in total and absolute awe of this imposing figure. The next thing I remember, is that I was fully awake but with the lingering presence of a Heavenly being. I then just tried to process what I had just experienced. The Lord God had sent His mightiest angel to protect me! That was an awesome feeling but also a humbling one. Why did the Lord send such a powerful angel to help me? I know that I pray the St. Michael prayer many times a day, so perhaps that's the reason.

My experiences with the other 2 Arch-Angels, St. Raphael and St. Gabriel, were just as profound as with St. Michael.

During my years in the prayer group, I received a very powerful vision of St. Raphael with a "mission" attached to it.

The "mission", was to lay hands on those who were ill, and pray for their healing through the intercession of St. Raphael. St. Raphael is often referred to as the "Medicine of God". The reason, is because in the book of Tobit, the Holy Angel Raphael heals Tobit of his blindness.

When I received this vision, St. Raphael appeared to me holding a flask of medicine, like he typically is depicted in his Holy Card. That was my indication, along with the inspiration of the Holy Spirit, that I needed to lay hands on the sick and pray for their healing. When the next prayer meeting after the vision occurred, I testified to the group on what I had received. I ended praying for many people that night, with many testifying the following week of healings they received through the "Medicine of God", including this older woman, who received the grace to be able to walk without the help of her walker, which she had been using for quite a while. Praise be to God!

My experience with St. Gabriel came in the form of a vision and the knowledge, that I was under his protection as well. That was such a powerful vision. To feel the presence of an Arch-Angel such as St. Gabriel, and to know that I was under his watch, was absolutely incredible to me. The Arch-Angel, who announced the birth of Christ to the Holy Virgin, was watching over me!

Just like with St. Michael and St. Raphael, the presence of St. Gabriel, was on another level all its own, in feeling these Heavenly visitors. Their presence had a grandiose feel to them, compared to a "regular" angel. I don't know if one should refer to an angel as regular, but these Arch-Angels were definitely something more than that! These Angels, are the ones who stand around the throne of God!

Chapter 11. The Holy Saints

A Saint, is a departed soul whom the Holy Catholic Church, officially recognizes as being in Heaven through the process of canonization. These men and women, and sometimes young children, led a life of heroic virtue during their lifetimes. The Church allows veneration of these Holy Souls and prayers of intercession through them. Many miracles have been attributed to their intercession.

I was immediately drawn to the Saints from the very first day my conversion. St. Faustina, played a very important part in my formation at the beginning of my journey. Re-reading her "Diary" for the 2nd time, I was truly amazed on how similar our mystical experiences where. When I read the "Diary" for the first time, I had no idea that what I was reading, was going to happen to me as well, in terms of the mysticism. Through St. Faustina, I gained a deep devotion to the Passion of Our Lord Jesus Christ, so much so, that I desired to receive the wounds of Christ, often referred to as stigmata. St. Faustina was granted the grace to suffer invisible stigmata, in which the physical wounds do not appear, only the pain of them. St. Francis of Assisi, St. Padre Pio and St. Gemma Galgani, are 3 of the Saints, who did suffer the physical stigmata.

I received the stigmata a few times in my dream. In one of those dreams, our young priest, the one who was moved to a new parish, was sitting across from our Bishop, who is now the bishop in California, and they were throwing dimes to each other. The dimes, had what looked like a very small bolt of lightning behind it, as it sailed across between the priest and bishop. I reached out to catch one of the dimes that were being tossed, and the lightening bolt, struck the palm of my hand, which then started to bleed. The pain was extreme. My thought immediately, was that I had received the stigmata. I just stared at pain-ridden hand as it was bleeding. When I awoke almost immediately at that point, the physical pain remained. The pain was now on both my hands, and on both my feet. This lasted for about half a day. This was a tremendous grace for me, to be given to feel the wounds of Our Lord, even though it was only a small fraction of His pain.

The mystical Saint, St. Gemma Galgani, was another Saint in whom I was very drawn to. In particular, because of her mystical experiences. The Saints with mystical experiences, were the only people who I could relate to during the first part of my conversion. St. Gemma's courage, in her supernatural dealings with the Evil One, was very edifying for me in terms of my own dealings with the Satan and his minions.

The other thing that fascinated me about St. Faustina and St. Gemma, was their love for God. I couldn't fully comprehend how someone could love God that much in midst of their tremendous physical and spiritual battles. I became envious of that. I wanted to love God as much as they did. Their expressions of love for God through their writings, was truly inspirational to me. That was very beneficial in my spiritual growth. My love for God began to increase by leaps and bounds. I realized that love was much more than a feeling, it was Jesus Christ Himself!

St. Therese of Lisieux, the Little Flower, was also very instrumental in my early development. I learned from her, that I did not need to achieve great feats in order to become a Saint, to become holy. There were smaller ways, the "little way" as she called it, to reach Heaven, to achieve sainthood. It was by doing the little things with great love.

The one Saint that has had the biggest impact on me thus far, is St. Padre Pio. This Capuchin Friar is the one Saint, in whom I call my spiritual father. St. Pio, had many spiritual children during his long holy life in a monastery in Southern Italy, in a town called Pietrelcina. This holy priest performed many miracles through his numerous spiritual gifts from God. Apart from his stigmata, in which he suffered for 50 years, he was well known for his work in the confessional. People would wait for days, even weeks, for a chance to go to confession with St. Pio. One of his many gifts was the gift of reading of souls. That gift, fascinating me more than any of his other gifts. As I recounted earlier, God through His Spirit, has granted me that gift, but I'm sure not to the extent of this holy man who was a Saint.

To "know", what a person has within their souls, makes me feel humble, it makes me feel love. To be granted this gift, the Lord allows me to see the core of who we are, our souls. The soul literally has the hand of God all over it. It is by our sins, by our choices, by are going away from God, that sullies our souls.

The humbleness of this great Saint, with all that he was given, is truly amazing. In contrast, I struggle so much with what I was given. It's very easy to fall into spiritual pride. St. Pio's example is what I look to in dealing with my spiritual pride.

I have had numerous profound dreams of St. Pio through the years. I know from reading through a multitude of testimonies of his life, St. Pio has appeared in the dreams of the faithful since his death in 1968, and many times during his lifetime as well. I know the Lord has allowed St. Pio, to communicate with through my dreams.

In one of my dreams of him, I went to confession with him. The confessional was in my house, in my living room. I was in a state of shock that I was about to enter the confessional with this holy man. The confessional, was the old-fashioned confessional that was employed by many churches many years ago. Some still use it to this day. It's a wooden structure that has the priest somewhat enclosed in the center, with the person confessing, on the kneeler on either side of the priest. The only thing that I remember aside from it being in my house, is walking up to the kneeler and then leaving the confessional. I do not remember what I confessed or what spiritual advice St. Pio gave me. When I awoke, I had an incredible sense of joy that I got to experience the confessional that so many people had the grace of, confessing to a saintly priest.

In another dream I had of St. Pio, I was in the house that I'm living in now, and St Pio appeared in his full priestly vestments. He was in my living room where I was, along with some members of my family as well. I was so excited that he appeared because in real life, I had been praying for confirmation on something very powerful that I had received.

I had received an impending death for a family that attended our prayer group. Whenever I receive something of this magnitude, much prayer goes into confirming the vision or message, or whatever it may be. I want to be 100% certain that what I receive, is first of all from God, and secondly, that it's not from an evil source. In this particular case, this wasn't the first time I had to deliver such a message of impending death to this particular family. Needless to say, I was very hesitant to pass along the message.

As soon as I realized that St. Pio had appeared in my dream, I directly go the Saint and ask him, "Padre Pio, Padre Pio isn't it true that what I received is correct?". Padre Pio then responded, "yes, yes it is correct", and with that, I woke up. I knew once again that the Lord had answered me through my spiritual father St. Padre Pio.

The other and most important dream I had of St. Pio, was a message for me.

The dream took place in his monastery in Italy. This was a couple of years before I was blessed of actually going to his monastery during my Italian pilgrimage in 2013.

When St. Padre Pio was alive, he received a multitude of pilgrims throughout his long life. St. Pio rarely left the monastery, and with the many pilgrims he received, it was very difficult to receive a personal blessing, or prayer from him because of the many visitors he had throughout his day. St. Pio would often tell the faithful to send him their Guardian Angels if they couldn't reach him personally. St. Pio could see and speak with his Angel and those of other people. There have been many testimonies of this being true, of people reaching St Pio through their Guardian Angels and having their prayers answered.

I arrived at the monastery in the dream, with my parents and my oldest sister. I first noticed a large crowd spilling out of one the monastery main rooms. The monastery itself was an old adobe styled structure.

The tan colored walls made the monastery look plain. We stood out in the foyer with a small group and I noticed within the crowd, that St. Pio was making his way through the swarming crowd. It seemed hopeless in trying to get some time alone with him, or much less see him. I quickly remembered about sending my Guardian Angel to him, so he could reach this holy man for me. I shut my eyes and began praying for my Angel to reach Padre Pio. Then all of a sudden, I see a brown hooded figure making his way back through the crowd, who were unaware that someone was making their way through them. All their focus was on trying to get into the main room and seeing this living Saint. As this brown cloaked figure was getting closer, I realized it was him, Padre Pio. No one had noticed that he made his way back to us. We were all excited, and we asked for him to pray for us. We all then knelt down. My family and I, were behind a few other people there, including a prostitute. I do not know how I knew that, but this blonde long-haired woman was there asking for a change in her life. St Pio, then proceeded to lay his hands on each person's head and gave a quick prayer and blessing. I was very anxious as he got closer to me. I was the last one in this prayer line. The Saint, finally got to me. I felt his hand on my head as I had my eyes closed, and at that moment, my consciousness went to another level. It felt like I was being transported to another place as well. I heard his voice deep within my soul and consciousness, and he said to me, "you will accomplish great things in this life, if you follow the will of God" and with that, while still dreaming, I opened my eyes, and I was back in my small town on the floor of our city council chambers. I noticed my hand as I was trying to get up, and I had a bunch of writing on it like someone had taken a pen to it. It was some type of writing that I did not recognize. There were some symbols as well, but I couldn't make it out. The writing then started to fade at a rapid pace. The reasoning that I received about the writing on the hand, was that it was from a demonic source. At that point, I woke up.

St. Padre Pio's words in this dream, became ingrained in my whole being. I was a bit nervous about this prophetic message, but also very excited as well at the notion that the Lord God, had many more things for me in the future. One of the first things that I did as I got up that morning, was to go look for an actual audio recording of St. Padre Pio's voice. I eventually found one on a website that was strictly devoted to him. This site included a ton of testimonies from the faithful, with writings and quotes from the holy priest as well. I finally came upon some video and some audio of him. The audio was of him praying. I quickly clicked on the link, and listened to this Saint pray in his native Italian language. His voice was exactly like the one I heard in my dream! The only difference, is that in the dream he had spoken English. I was elated, because once again the Lord spoke to me through my dreams, through Saint Padre Pio!

This message brought with it a bit of a burden on me after some time. What sort of "great things" am I going to accomplish? What is God asking of me? These were the questions I kept asking myself over and over again. Only God knew at that point in my life what was is store for me. It wasn't until 2016, that I realized that dream had come to pass.

The multitude of souls that the Lord God has allowed me to pray for mercy, before their deaths, is what Padre Pio was referring to in the dream. It was after the suicide, that I wrote about earlier that took place in May of 2016, that I fully realized that the dream had come true. It was the accomplishing of God's will and not my own, that the great things came. It wasn't any selfish personal goals that I had originally thought it to be. His Mercy, allowed these great things to be accomplished, namely the salvation of a legion of souls through prayer. I pray that many more great things are accomplished through His will in the future. Praise be to God and His Mercy!

There have been other Saints, in which I've taken something from them and applied it to my own life. Each one of them helped me in my formation in key times throughout these first 10 years.

Two of these Saints, St. Teresa of Avila and St. John of the Cross, who were 16th century Spanish Saints, through their lives and writings, helped me understand what was happening within my soul. From the darkness and purification that St. John wrote about, to the many levels of growth of the soul from St. Teresa.

The holy Saints of the Catholic Church, are there to help us all on our way to salvation. From the humility and example of love of St. Francis of Assisi, to the bravery and courage and sacrifice of St. Maximilian Kolbe, the Saint of Auschwitz, and to the dedication of serving the sick from Blessed Francis Xavier Seelos.

Each Saint in their unique way can contribute to each of us in our uniqueness. There is one though, that stands above all the Saints to whom the Lord gave us from His Cross. She is the most helpful, and sure way for us, to get to Heaven and that person is the Blessed Virgin Mary.

Chapter 12. The Queen of Heaven

The Queen of Heaven, Tower of Ivory, Mystical Rose, Mirror of Justice, Our Lady of Guadalupe, Our Lady of Lourdes, Our Lady of Fatima, Our Mother, My Mother, all these titles are all one in the same person, the Blessed Virgin Mary.

Outside from our Lord's infinite mercy upon me, the prayers and intercessions of Our Lady are what saved my life as well. I've consecrated myself to her most Immaculate Heart. She has been very instrumental in guiding me and leading me on this journey.

I've been praying the Holy Rosary for as long as I can remember. Growing up, we'd pray it before mass every May and October, the months dedicated to Our Lady. Our old priest Father Nagle, had a huge devotion to her. That is one of the reasons why, and plus our church is named after one of her titles, Our Lady of Lourdes. Our catechism classes when I was growing up, also prayed the Rosary on Mary's Months. My knowledge of her was limited in my younger years, to the Rosary and what I knew about the Nativity, the birth of Christ. It was like that for a large part of my life. It wasn't until my conversion, that my thirst for knowledge about her grew. I believe I was like most Catholics I knew, in terms of our knowledge of Our Lady. I didn't fully know the story about our namesake either. I was so ignorant of the rich history of the Catholic Church.

When my conversion happened, I became like a sponge and I tried to soak up as much information as I could about the Church and her history.

As my conversion started, I began to pray the Rosary every day, but this time I prayed it with purpose, with an understanding of what I was praying, the life of Jesus Christ through His mother.

2008 was the year that my relationship with Our Lady became something otherworldly.

There was one experience in 2006 though, that involved Our Lady.

That experience, was on the same night when I was prayed for, before I went to tell the "girl" about the first vision of death that I had, that involved her unborn child.

When some members of the prayer group prayed over me, as I had my eyes closed, I saw a blueish colored fabric, cover my entire mind's eye. Instead of seeing the dark shadows that I wrote about in the original story of the "girl", I saw Our Lady's blue mantle covering me. I knew it was her, by the "knowledge" that the Lord had given me. She was showing me that she was protecting me. It wasn't until 2 years later, that her presence became a constant in my life. In the Summer of 2008, a dream of her, started my supernatural journey with the Queen of Heaven.

In this very profound dream, I was running down a hill that was very steep. I was running which seemed like I was running for my life, with about 5 or 6 other people.

We were being chased by some unseen force. The only thing we could see, is that everything in the path of this great force, was turning into rock. Nothing in its path escaped this frightening change. The trees, the ground beneath us, and every little thing around us, turned to rock. We were all able to make it into an old mobile home, figuring we were safe from this terror. As we were catching our breath from running for our lives, this evil force entered the mobile home and started overtaking every object within seconds. I stood there motionless seeing everything turn into rock. It overtook the people whom I had run with as well. The person next to me, had a mug in his hand when this force consumed him. I saw him change from human flesh to solid rock. It consumed him starting from his feet and rose quickly to the top of his head. It even changed the mug he was holding to rock as well. He stood there now, as everything else in it's path did, lifeless. The force approached me just as fast as it did the man next to me, but in an instant, a light covered me. This evil force was unable to harm me as he did the others. I looked around and I saw one other person being protected by this light, it was one of my nieces. She is the second daughter of my second oldest sister. She was just 13 at the time of this dream. We both looked at each other, and then we simultaneously looked at the light protecting us that was coming right through the ceiling above us. We quickly went outside to see where the source of this light was coming from. Above this old and very dirty mobile home, the source of this light was that of the Blessed Virgin Mary. The light was so bright that I couldn't see her, but my soul knew that it was her splendor that was protecting us and with that, I woke up with and incredible sense of peace. The sense of peace as always, being typical of a sign of it being a dream from Above. In this case, being from the Holy Virgin.

The next morning at Mass, I was invited along with some of my family, to a house of a couple who also attended our prayer group. This Hispanic couple revealed to me, that the husband while at work at a ranch, came upon a large stone that was somehow split perfectly in half. What appeared in the middle of the rock on both parts, was an image of Our Lady!

This couple had invited our young priest at the time, to their house after mass to bless the image, and to also pray the Holy Rosary with them and some of their extended family.

I immediately connected this dream to this couple, because they lived in a mobile home very similar to the one from the dream, plus this connection with Our Lady and the image. The Holy Spirit confirmed to me that this dream was true and from her. I was so excited and my heart was full of joy, knowing that the Mother of God was communicating with me!

That joyful day also had a very tragic part to it as well.

Before we had to go to the Rosary, we attended a funeral of a baby that died in the womb of this young girl. This young girl, who was around 5 months pregnant, lost her baby after having some complications. This young girl and her mother, went to one of our weekly prayer meetings about a month prior to the baby's death, to ask for prayers for the baby whom the doctors said was forming with severe problems.

This girl was around 17 at the time and I was told that her mother had on occasion attended the prayer meetings before my time there. It was very common for people within our parish and some outside the parish, to come to the prayer meetings to ask for prayers for healing, or whatever problem they were having. This was one of the duties of the group. The group, or certain members of the group, also went out to wherever they were needed to pray.

We placed the young girl that night, within our large prayer circle and we began to pray for her. My father took lead as he always did. My mother and I joined in along with a couple of senior members of the group as well.

With all that I was receiving from God at the time, I knew the Lord would hear my prayers for this girl. My spiritual pride was telling me that my prayers, were more effective than others because I was "in touch" with Heaven through all the gifts I had received up to that point. I was very naive at that time about that. I did pray with everything I had though. I couldn't sense anything as I prayed over this young girl. I didn't know at that moment, that the Lord had already shown me something about that night until later.

When we first got the news of the death of the baby, I felt heartbroken. Foremost for the girl and her loss and secondly, because I thought I had failed her. I blamed myself for not praying hard enough for her. I felt that I should've been able to pray enough for this girl's baby to be healed and to be born healthy. Again, my spiritual pride was blinding me.

These spiritual gifts did not make me any better than anyone else, or more privileged than anyone else, and this was one of the situations that taught me that. These gifts were given to me to serve God and others and not for my selfishness.

The funeral on that mid-summer day, was attended by a very few people. Her large family made up a lot of the attendance. At the cemetery, I didn't feel much in terms of picking up other people's emotions. Perhaps part of my mind was focused on what was going to happen after the funeral, the Rosary and the blessing of the image at the couple's home with our priest. I did feel a deep sadness for the young girl though, and as we gave our condolences, I whispered to her that she would be in my prayers. I've prayed for her daily ever since.

A couple of days after the funeral, as I was writing in my journal, I read the entry that I wrote on the day the young girl first showed up to be prayed for. The entry started with the dream I had the night before. In this dream, I was at our Church and I was sitting with a bunch of young people, including a couple of my nieces. It was a funeral mass that we were attending in the dream. One of my nieces in the dream was a schoolmate of the young girl who lost her child. It was at that moment that the Lord God had allowed me to know that the dream, was the future event of this young girl's baby's funeral. The same two nieces in the dream, attended the actual funeral as well because of their acquaintance of the young girl and her sister. I realized, that I was given that dream so I could pray for the soul of the person, and for the family of the person who was going to die, and in this case, the girl's unborn child.

I don't pretend to understand God's ways in this case. When we prayed for the unborn child and young mother the month before, it was already known by God that the baby wasn't going to live. The prayers, the dream, it was all for the young girl. It was for the grace for her to deal with this impending tragedy and not for the healing of her child.

I've seen this young girl on many occasions since that day of the funeral, and I know she still has pain from that tragic loss. God has blessed her though with two more babies since the death of her first child. Perhaps, that's what the prayers in 2008 were for as well. Every time I see her now though, I'm still reminded of that tragedy.

After the funeral, we made our way to the mobile home of the couple from the prayer group, to pray the Rosary. The mobile home was about a few minutes away from the cemetery that was located in the south part of our small town. We were greeted by the couple and by some of their extended family as we arrived on that hot mid-July day. We were taken around to the outside of the home, where they had set up to have the Rosary prayed. It was the late afternoon by now, and so we were in the shade. It was still extremely warm as we sat down on the dining room chairs that they had brought out from the inside of their home. We were then shown the split rock of the image of Our Lady as we waited for our young priest to arrive. The image in the split rock was undeniably that of Our Lady. It was a side profile picture that one usually sees of the Holy Virgin Mary, veil and all. It was truly amazing.

A couple of weeks before all this, I had been reading a book by Blessed Anne Catherine Emmerich. It was about her incredible visions of the life of the Holy Virgin Mary. Blessed Anne, was a German nun from the late 18th century and early 19th century. She had these incredible mystical experiences that included visions of the Passion of our Lord Jesus Christ, and of the life of Mary Magdalene and the one book I was reading, "The Life of the Holy Virgin Mary". The visions of Blessed Anne were incredible. The Lord had given Blessed Anne, the incredible gift of seeing in vision, the day to day life of the Holy Virgin Mary. Everything was written in detail about the Virgin Mary, from the clothes that she was wearing, to the house she lived in after the Resurrection of our Lord, and to the last day the Holy Mother spent on Earth and her eventual Assumption into Heaven. I guess the Holy Spirit had begun to pique my interest in the Holy Virgin, a few weeks prior to the vision I was about to receive of her.

Our priest finally arrived, and we quickly got into the whole reason of being there, the Holy Virgin Mary. He was shown the image, which was propped up on a makeshift altar, ready for veneration. The young priest was genuinely amazed by the image, in which he proceeded to bless along with all of us there as well. We then began to pray the Holy Rosary. We prayed the Glorious Mysteries, which is typical for a Sunday. We prayed it in Spanish, in which our non-Hispanic priest was fluent in. I don't remember which Mystery of the Rosary we were on, when the Lord granted me a very powerful vision.

I felt a Heavenly presence, and my eyes began to tear up. Tears were a sign that the Heavenly presence I was given to feel, to sense, was from God. The tears, which seemed to start on their own and not by my doing, is often referred to as the "gift of tears". This has occurred on many occasions. It's not a natural occurrence of tears brought on by sorrow or joy, but brought on by a spiritual experience of God.

I "saw" a woman very clearly as I was in the midst of this "gift of tears". I saw that her hair was of a reddish brown color. This woman was looking down. The details of her face, were for hidden from me for some reason, but in my heart, I knew that this was the Blessed Virgin Mary! I tried my best to control these "tears", but I couldn't. We finished the Rosary, and I didn't share with anyone what I had just been given to see. No one said anything to me about the "tears", which I thought was so obvious to everyone there, or at least to those near me. Perhaps they didn't notice or perhaps, they thought I just got emotional. Whatever the case, my heart was bursting with joy knowing that I had just experienced a taste of Heaven!

The first thing I did when I got back home, after this long and spiritually up and down and then up again day, was to find my book on the "Life of the Blessed Virgin Mary" that I was reading. I quickly flipped through it to find a description of the Holy Mother given by Blessed Anne through her powerful visions. I found it pretty quickly. Blessed Anne described the Queen of Heaven with having her hair being of a reddish-brown color. Confirmation! My heart was once again filled with this immense joy. My only question was why was I given this to see. I quickly received an answer to that in a few weeks time.

A very short period after that incredible day, I had been given to deliver "messages" to people within the prayer group. This took place over the span of two weeks or so.

These "messages" from Above, were nothing new at that point, but the incredible frequency of them was. I would receive these "messages", at all hours of the day and for most of them, I was not even in prayer. The way I would receive the "messages", began with the intended person, just randomly flashing through my mind. Then I would keep them in my mind at that point and this understanding of what needed to be given to them, was just infused in my thoughts. I may have written some of these "messages" down somewhere, just to keep track of them, only because of the sheer number of them.

When the next prayer meeting would come around, I gave the "message", to the intended person. Sometimes, the message was their need to approach certain Saints for their intercession of what they were asking the Lord for through their prayers. Many times, the person would comment to the rest of the group on their amazement of the accuracy of the "message". I knew this was nothing of my doing though, but that tends to get lost a lot of the time. It's sometimes hard for people to truly comprehend that the supernatural is working and that God is working through us and among us. Praise be His Holy Name!

For some reason, after passing along all these "messages", I wanted a "message" for myself. It was probably my pride seeking this, but I wanted someone to come up to me, and give me something that was from God like I had been given to do for others. I guess I was also seeking some more confirmation, showing me that what I was doing was His will.

By the time August came along, my first pilgrimage to France was already set for October. My research on Our Lady and her apparitions in Lourdes was well underway. My devotion to her, was growing more and more with each passing day, and with each Rosary that I prayed.

It was on a Saturday, on a hot and muggy August day, that my wanting of a "message" was answered. It was in the early afternoon, that I received this inspiration to go to the Church and pray in front of Our Lord ever present in the Tabernacle. The Lord had allowed me to know, that there was a "message" awaiting me from Our Lady. I quickly showered and shaved, and went with great anticipation to the Church.

Just 2 weeks prior to this at the prayer meeting, I had the most profound experience with Our Lady. This was about a month after the first vision of her. It was after the Holy Hour we spent with Our Lord in the church that Our Lady came to me. We were back in the parish hall after that Holy Hour, when this occurred. I asked one of the musicians, to play a song dedicated to Our Lady as we entered into some deeper prayer time. I had already begun tearing up as I felt her presence there. The vision of her covering me with her mantle, is when I started to cry uncontrollably. It was her presence, her love, her splendor, that affected me as well. I remember that my mind and my tears were on two separate planes. I couldn't understand why I couldn't stop crying. It was like something was controlling it but at the same time, the feeling of her presence was overwhelming my heart and my soul. I don't think I've ever cried that much in my entire adult life. I know that the Holy Mother was there with me that night.

I started to pray the Rosary in order to receive my "message", and then in the middle of 2nd Glorious Mystery, I felt the presence of Our Lady and I began to tear up. I finished praying, and nothing, I didn't receive anything. I then moved to the front pew from where I was praying, which was a kneeler close to the altar, and I knelt down once again. I again asked the Holy Virgin for the "message", I offered her five more Hail Mary's for this, and by the time I got to the 3rd one, she made her presence fully known to me. It was very similar to how I felt at the prayer meeting I just described. The tears were flowing down my face at this point. When I finished the last of the 5 Hail Mary's, I heard the words, "Be faithful! Be faithful!". I was stunned because it was an audible voice that I heard. "Did I just hear her speak to me?", I thought to myself. My heart was beating 1000 miles per hour now. I heard the words clearly, like someone human, would be speaking right next to me. She was asking me to be faithful on what the Lord had for me, meaning the numerous trials I was to come upon in the future. I asked for confirmation that this, was from her and not my imagination, or from some evil source. I asked her to wrap me in her holy mantle once again, as proof that all of this was truly from her. I offered her one Hail Mary for this grace, and when I had finished it, I felt this incredible warmth come over me. I felt this incredible feeling of protection over me as well.

I also felt this embrace that words can not suffice in describing it. I was in Heaven! Thank you Mother Mary!

That began my "communication" with the Queen of Heaven, which still continues to this day.

The next couple of months, leading up to my pilgrimage to France, were filled with many visions of Our Lady. This was accompanied by many words from her as well. Her words, were of love and encouragement and of hope, and of things to come. After the first couple of years of my conversion, that were filled with some much of the evil one and some very dark visions, these Heavenly visions were such a blessing in my life. It came at the perfect time.

This grace of Our Lady and her "communications", were beyond anything I could've imagine at that point in my "life". Thank you Holy Virgin!

One of the main stops of the 2008 French pilgrimage, was Lourdes. The vast majority of our group, were made up of parishioners from my parish. Our young priest at the time had organized this trip, being that it was the 150th anniversary of the apparitions of Our Lady to St. Bernadette Soubirous in 1858.

I was anticipating feeling all sorts of spiritual and Heavenly presences throughout the trip, since we were visiting all the main Catholic sites throughout France. We visited the Notre Dame Cathedral in Paris, which was incredible, but I didn't feel anything supernatural. The same thing with the Sacre Couer basilica in Paris, it was beautiful, but nothing supernatural. It was still an incredible blessing none the less. Same thing at

Normandy Beach, I didn't feel the loss of life there either, but then again, it was super cold and windy when we visited this monumental landmark. I did feel something however in Lisieux, when we visited the home of St.Therese the Little Flower and her incredible Basilica. The feeling was otherworldly with her Holy Relics being there, but it was nothing compared to what was awaiting for me in Lourdes. What I felt and experienced there, surpassed all my expectations and more.

When our group arrived in Lourdes, it was in the middle of the night and so needless to say, we were all tired. It wasn't till the mid-morning, that we were led out to the holy spot to where Our Mother appeared. As soon as we walked through one of the gates that lead into the Basilica and church grounds, I felt her presence there. The closer we got to the Grotto where she appeared, the stronger her presence got. The whole property where all this lies, is by the Pyrenees mountains. The whole area was so picturesque.

It was rainy and cold in the beginning but it didn't damper our spirits. There are multiple churches that make up this holy pilgrimage site, and we got to tour and attend mass in a couple of them. These European cathedrals and basilicas, are so incredibly beautiful, I wish that everyone of the Catholic faithful back home, could see what we did on that trip, and on my subsequent trips. The architectural designs of all of them were majestic and awe-inspiring. It was very spiritually uplifting to visit them all in person.

We got to be fully immersed in the miraculous water via the baths there by the Grotto, where countless pilgrims have gone seeking miracles of all sorts. Many souls have come away with healings of both the physical and in most cases, and probably most importantly, spiritual.

Ironically, I had no ills of either sort at this point but shortly after my return back home, the first signs of being diabetic came about. At times, I've wondered that if perhaps I picked up someone's illness while I was there. I've been given to experience things like that in the past by the Lord and perhaps this disease, was one of these times. Only He knows for certain.

We were given some free time on our own while we were there in Lourdes, and I spent most of it praying in front of the Grotto. I saw this young man there with his head down praying so intently, asking Our Lady for help. I looked at him and then I looked at all the people there, a lot of them, had their eyes fixed on the statue of the Holy Virgin standing in the exact spot where she appeared 150 years earlier and I felt so unworthy. I was thinking,"why did I get blessed with these incredible visions and "communications" with her and not them?”. Any one of these pilgrims would've given anything to "see" and "hear" and to "talk" with Our Lady like I had been granted. "Why did God pick me for this?" I asked myself. "My Devotion to her was no greater than theirs, and probably in a lot of cases, a lot less than theirs". These thoughts ran through my mind while looking upon all these faithful souls there and also many times throughout the first 10 years of this "life".

I had my backpack with me as I prayed there in front of Our Lady, and in my backpack I carried written petitions from most of the people from the prayer group. There was a reason I had them with me, it was because the Holy Virgin asked for it.

The month prior to our trip, what I was receiving from Our Lady was becoming very powerful. These inspirations I received from her, were always confirmed by her when our "communications" occurred. One of these inspirations that was confirmed by her, was of her seeking written petitions from the faithful. She wanted to grant us through her intercession, what we asked from her through these petitions. She asked that we have a devotion to the most Holy Rosary in return. The Rosary, is what will draw us closer to her and that in turn, would lead us ultimately to her Son Jesus Christ. She would lead us to Him through the Rosary. The Rosary will unite us, bring those who have strayed away from Christ and the Church, back. It will bring unity and peace to our families. It would bring healing of all sorts for those who asked her through the Rosary. It was all contingent on the Rosary. I stressed the Rosary many times over and over again to the prayer group. On a Thursday just shortly prior to our trip, I revealed and testified to the prayer group, everything that I had begun to receive from the Holy Virgin Mary, including her seeking the petitions. She said that she would call upon me and ask me to bring the petitions to her. Most all of the prayer group, save a few, wrote down their petitions and I kept them with me untill the day she called me to bring them to her, which ended up being a little later down the line.

During the evening times in Lourdes, a candlelight Rosary procession takes place. Our Lady told St Bernadette 150 years earlier, that she wanted people to come to her in procession, and the people did. Millions upon millions of people over the years did.

It was cold as we gathered in front of the main Basilica waiting for the start of the procession. Most of the group was able to come out and take part in it. We all had our candles with wind protectors, which had the Hail Mary printed on it in 4 different languages. The organizers then brought out a lighted platform with a huge lighted statue of Our Lady in the center. It was carried about by 4 men. This platform of Our Lady led the procession. We then began to walk as the Rosary was started. Each mystery was prayed in a different language. It was prayed in English, French, Spanish, and 2 others languages I don't quite remember, but it was prayed beautifully nonetheless. It was beautiful seeing so many pilgrims praying in their native tongue. It was so awesome! My heart and soul were being illuminated by all of it. We processed around the grounds of this Marian apparition sight making our way back to where we started. Loudspeakers that were aligned throughout the grounds, made the hearing of the prayers very clear as we honored the Holy Virgin. As we got close to the end of the procession, as the "Ave Maria's" rang out from the chorus of the hymn "Immaculate Mary", my soul once again heard the voice of the Queen of Heaven! She said to me, "you will receive whatever you ask of me". I heard these words as loud as the throngs of people's voices were in singing to the Holy Mother! The pure love and joy that were in my heart and soul of feeling and hearing Our Lady, once again allowed me to have a taste of Heaven. If it were possible for my heart to explode with all the happiness it felt at that moment, I believe it would've happened right there. Thank you Holy Mother!

I also knew at that moment, that she was asking more of me as well. I believed that she wanted what was happening in Lourdes, and at the other Marian Shrines around the world, to come to my town, to Mineral Wells. I was steadily discerning this as pilgrimage came along, and this incredible moment at the "Torchlight Procession", made it clear to me that it was exactly what she wanted. All I needed now was more confirmation.

The impact on my soul from that first trip to Lourdes has stayed with me even to this day but now, I had to ask the Holy Virgin for confirmation on what she was asking of me.

Soon after we arrived back home, I began to piece together everything that I had received in such a short time since that vision on that hot July day in 2008.

I knew in order for the things that the Holy Virgin was asking of us all to be done, our parish priest had to be involved.

It was one thing telling believers about the supernatural, such as the prayer group, it's totally another thing telling our young parish priest about it. How would he receive all this? Would he think I was crazy? I honestly did not know how he would react, and so I asked the Holy Mother for a physical sign. The physical sign would leave no doubt for me or to anyone else, that what I was receiving was truly from Heaven. I believed it all to be true with all my heart, but I needed to have confirmation. I had read online about hoaxes and false apparitions, and about false visions that people had, claiming to have seen and to have heard the Holy Virgin. This was a big reason I asked for the sign to be a physical one. I offered Our Lady a Rosary for the sign. I spelled out everything to her, making sure that what I had been given to discern, was correct and of her. A day and a half later, she gave me what I asked for, my sign!

My mom called me and said that she had found something outside the house while she was picking flowers. I go outside to see what it was, and she shows me a rock. "What do you see?" she asked me. My heart almost jumped out my chest when I saw the rock. It was an image of Our Lady on the rock! I could clearly see the whole outline and shape of Our Lady with her mantle and with her hands folded. It was very similar to many images one sees of the Holy Mother. I was stunned. I then told my mother what I was praying for, the sign. Then the realization that I had received something so incredibly profound hit me. The visions, her voice, her presence, everything was truly real! The image on the rock somehow made everything more serious to me, in regards to what I was receiving. It made me understand the gravity of it as well. I had been granted the grace to speak and to see the Mother of God! I quickly called the church office and made an appointment to see the priest and tell him what the Blessed Mother was asking. The young priest said he could meet with me the next day. I prayed for guidance the rest of that day in preparation for the meeting.

I arrived at the church office the next day a bit nervous, but with the renewed confidence of what I had been receiving from Our Lady. I started with my testimony up to that point, and then I went into everything I had received from her. I then said to the priest at that point, "she says if you don't accept all this, and say no, then it all ends here. She said it's in your hands". I told him about her wanting the processions and what effect the Rosary can have if the people believe and devote themselves to it and to her. I told him that she wants to be here with us as she had been throughout the world at her approved apparition sites. I finally finished explaining everything to him, and then he told me his thoughts. "First of all", he said, "I don't think you're crazy", he said this with a slight chuckle. I was relieved by that. He continued saying that I had appeared to have properly "tested the spirits" as we were told to do in 1 John 4:1. He finished saying that he was going to pray on it and get back to me with a decision. I figured it was a lot for him to digest. He hadn't been a priest very long at that point, and so I assumed that he hadn't directly heard anything like what I told him that mid-November morning. He had mentioned earlier though, that his confessor while he was in the seminary, was Charismatic. With that fact, I knew he was familiar with the Charisms, spiritual gifts, that I had spoken to him about. He even mentioned once during morning mass, that is confessor would sometimes "speak in tongues", which is a spiritual gift, during his confessions with him.

The next morning at daily mass, he didn't say anything to me about his decision and that made me a little nervous, but I trusted that Our Lady was working on this. The following morning after mass, I asked him what his decision was and he said that he had spoken to the Bishop about it. The Bishop said that the procession would be OK to do, but not on a daily basis like I had said the Holy Mother wanted. The Bishop said it would lose something if it was done everyday, that it would become routine. He said it would be a good thing for the parish to do, but he didn't give us a day when we could actually have one. I knew the Holy Virgin would help us in getting it approved! The only thing though, we are called to pray the Rosary every day and so I don't think that doing it in a daily procession would ever become routine, but I humbly submitted to the Bishop's and our priest's decision on this. Praise be to God!

I gave the good news to my family and to the group during the next prayer meeting. I was so excited about this new journey that I was about to start with the Mother of God!

About a month went by, and there was nothing from our priest about the processions. I had some more "communications" with Our Lady during this time though, and she gave me more to tell the priest. I thought these new visions to communicate back to him were a perfect opportunity to bring up the procession once again.

I went to confession on a Saturday night right before Mass, as this is the usual time that our parish holds this Sacrament. I confessed and then I brought up the new message right before I was about to leave. I told our young priest, "the Lady said to tell the priest that he won't be able to enter our town (Mineral Wells), and not encounter someone who's not here for her.", meaning what she promised would come, if we devoted ourselves to her and the Holy Rosary. The "knowledge" of what would come, was given to me to tell him as well. The changes of hearts, full conversions, and people from other faiths would also join the Catholic

Church. The curious would be converted as well. People from all over would come to see what was happening here, the appearing of Our Lady. She said miracles would come to those who believed. Once again, all this, was to lead us to her son Jesus Christ.

I kept seeing all this play out in visions. I would see the streets around our church jammed packed with people processing around behind a statue of Our Lady like in Lourdes. There were times during these visions, I felt as though I was truly there present among the people. It was like I was transported to these future events, I could see everything very clearly. These visions always brought me to tears.

Our priest, after I relayed all this to him, just repeated "we will do the processions", but again gave no time frame.

I delivered the last message, and with that my job was done. It was now in the hands of the young priest once more.

The Holy Virgin, then sought to have Rosaries prayed in the houses of those who believed in what I was given from her. Specifically, it was for those in the prayer group. I then brought this message to the group. We had like 8 or 9 families sign up for this incredible grace. We made a schedule and then my parents and I, began this new work for Our Lady.

The Blessed Mother promised me through my many visions and "talks" with her, that all I needed to do was invoke her presence, and she would appear to me during the Rosary. I tested this out as well, to make sure that this wasn't my imagination or from an evil source. Once again, the Blessed Mother confirmed all this to me by appearing to me like she had promised, as I invoked her presence during the Holy Rosary.

This isn't a case where the Holy Mother is at my beck and call. I believe that she is always present when we faithfully pray the Most Holy Rosary. She had just granted me the grace to see her, and to hear her, when we do. It is something that I take with a lot of gratitude. Again, this grace doesn't make me any better or special because of it. It's just something that I was given to help bring souls to God through the Holy Virgin.

The whole process of the "Special Rosary", in which I called it, began with an explanation of how she appears to me and then the Rosary is prayed. The laying of hands then proceeded the Rosary. Most of the time, she has "messages" for whomever I am praying for. Then we would finish with testimony on whatever was received during the whole "Special Rosary".

The Blessed Mother would often appear to me after the 2nd mystery. The "gift of tears" would accompany her appearance. She has appeared to me in many of her different titles. She has appeared as Our Lady of Lourdes, Our Lady of Fatima, Our Lady of Guadalupe and also as Our Lady of Mt Carmel. There were other titles that she appeared as, that I didn't recognize initially, but I knew it was her nonetheless. She at times has appeared with the Holy Angels and at other times, with some of the Holy Saints as well. It was such an incredible experience every time we held these "Special Rosaries".

I would let the family know the exact moment she had made herself seen to me. It was often very difficult to get this out because of the tears, and because the overwhelming feelings I was experiencing. There were some who received physical healing and there were some, who received other graces like visions of Our Lady as well. Many felt her presence through this "Special Rosary". Heaven, made its presence felt at each house we went to. What an incredible blessing!

All this was very draining for me, because a lot of spiritual preparations went into each "Special Rosary" we went to. I still had to work as well on top of that. We also did this "Special Rosary" on consecutive nights. It was all very worth it though. It was all for the glory of God! Thank you Holy Mother!

My parents were a huge support during this period with Our Lady. I can't thank them enough for that. They prayed so beautifully at each house we were blessed to visit.

We did the "Special Rosary" multiple times with the prayer group as well on our Thursday night meetings. The graces were abundant. Many people were prayed for during these incredible occasions. We saw a marriage reconciled, we saw some physical and spiritual healing take place among the group, through the intercession of the Holy Virgin. To experience the Rosary in this way with a large group of people, was absolutely incredible.

One particular time when we prayed this "special" way, someone gave testimony afterwards, that during the Rosary, the friend that she had brought with her that night, kept asking her if she smelled roses. He asked her if she was wearing rose scented perfume, because it seemed like it was all around. This young woman said to him that she wasn't, that no one was. This was another sign from Our Lady,! The scent of roses, was showing us that she was there among us.

This phenomenon occurred twice with me while I was praying the Rosary. Both times I was in the Church praying alone. The first time, I got up and searched the whole church looking for where the roses where placed, not realizing it was the scent of Our Lady. The second time, I knew it was her immediately. There were absolutely no roses in the Church on both occasions

This rose scented occurrence at the prayer group, along with the two times I was alone in the Church, confirmed to me that our praying this "way", was in fact fueled from Above.

All this took place in 2009 and all the while nothing from our priest on the processions. I asked him one final time during a Summer picnic that he Church sponsored. The heat from a Texas Summer day can be ruthless, and on that day, it was no exception. I approached our priest at a moment when he was alone. Some parishioners had asked him some church related questions a little earlier, and so I knew that my approaching him wasn't inappropriate in inquiring about the processions. I quickly went through what had been happening since the last time I spoke to him about Our Lady, and he seemed to react with a little doubt now. It was mainly because of the frequency of her appearances. It wasn't something that he said about it specifically, it was his body language and his facial expression. It also appeared to me that he couldn't quite comprehend it all. I guess he couldn't fully understand the why and the how, something like that could be happening here or possibly to someone like me. He did say though, that we would have the processions on the major Marian feast days that the Catholic Church celebrates throughout the year. That was good enough for me, especially after all the inaction that happened between my first bringing it all up to him, and that hot Summer day in the park. I thanked him and passed along the news to several prayer group members who were attending the picnic as well.

About a year went by, and the young priest didn't keep to his word. Nothing was done. In July of 2010, he was moved to another parish. On August 2010, the new priest, our current Indian priest, Father B., gave us permission to have our first full Church procession. The feast day of The Assumption of The Holy Virgin Mary into Heaven, is when it took place.

Was it Divine Providence that moved the young priest away? I don't know, but this new young priest was very spiritual and very open to the supernatural. Many more processions took place in the following years after the young priest left to another parish. Perhaps the Holy Virgin had something to do with the moving of the priest in order for God's will to be done.

Sometime before we began the "Special Rosaries", I had finally received the "call" from the Holy Mother to bring her the written petitions that I had in my backpack.

I was about to take a nap when this strong internal feeling came to me. It was not the typical "disturbances" that I receive when it's something evil or when it's death, but it was something from God. In this particular case, it was from Our Lady. I "understood", that she was calling for the petitions, and that she wanted them to be brought to the Church. I very quickly got dressed and I grabbed my backpack and I made the 7-minute drive to the Church. I was alone there, which was very good considering what was about to occur. I took out the light blue folder which held the petitions, and I asked the Blessed Mother what was I to do next. I prayed first of course, and I got myself spiritually ready. The Blessed Mother then asked for me to read each one of them to her, and to help offer them up on their behalf, and so that's what I did. There were 5 petitions that she wanted specifically to be read first. That instruction was given to me many months before. One of those petitions that was read first was that of my niece, who was in the first dream of Our Lady in which we were both protected by her light.

All 5 people in whose petitions were to be first, took the whole testimony I had of Our Lady with great faith. They were very humble and gracious in Our Lady's request.

As I read each petition to Our Lady, I felt as though I took on that person's hopes and supplications to her, as though I was the one who wrote down each petition. I seemed to have cried through each one of the 50 pages of petitions I read off and offered up to Our Lady. I really don't remember anything that was written on the 50 pages that I read to the Holy Mother. There may be a line or so that I can recall, but that was it. I destroyed the petitions when I came back home from that incredible experience. Her presence was very strong there in the Church. I know that the Holy Mother took each one of those petitions into her Immaculate Heart, and then interceded for us before her Son. I have no doubt about that. I honestly do not know if any of those petitions were answered though. Based on my constant preaching of the Rosary to them, and imploring them to take up praying it daily, many still didn't. Once again, I did what was asked of me. I can't force anyone to do something they don't want to do. There were some though, who just didn't believe as I stated earlier about that. It comes with the territory so to speak.

The processions we did with the new priest were special, but it wasn't done with the understanding that Our Lady would make herself appear to me. I was very hesitant to approach our new Indian priest as I did our last priest. The negativity that was left by the situation I talked about earlier, the dismantling of the prayer group, the meeting that he had with me where I had to defend myself, and my illness, all played a part in that. I did feel the presence of Our Lady when we did the processions though. Some people in attendance even commented later that they felt her presence as well during these processions.

The one we did in 2015 on the Feast of the Assumption, was the closest one to the "Special Rosary" since we started doing them. Her presence was very powerful on that occasion. Many people came to me afterwards and thanked me for organizing the procession. It was nothing of my doing though, it was the Blessed Mother.

One of the reasons for writing this book, is for the Holy Mother. It's for people to know what is happening in my small town. That her powerful and loving presence is here, and that a multitude of the graces await for us here if we believe.

There was a story that was told to me after I began receiving and discerning what the Holy Mother had for us.

The story involves our old Irish priest Father Nagle. It was said, that he saw an apparition of the Holy Virgin outside our Church as he was walking close by. He was frightened by it for some reason. Perhaps it was because it was so unexpected. They said that the apparition was the reason why he had such a strong devotion to her. When I heard this story, it just further confirmed to me that the presence of the Mother of God was strong here. She has always been here with us. It just took many years for her to make herself seen again.

One of the last confirmations I received about the Holy Virgin and everything that came with it, came from an unexpected person.

In late October of 2014, a lady that I knew from one of our jobs, showed up to help with a project the youth group from our Church was doing. I had been helping out with the youth group for about 5 years at that point. I spoke to this lady after we were done with the project, and we ended up talking for about 3 hours.

She told me about the spiritual experiences that she was having, which were similar to what I had gone through in my early years. Some of the things she described, were eerily similar in terms of my description of them. The thing that really struck me profoundly though, was her saying that something was coming to our town of Mineral Wells. She said that people from all over would be drawn here by it. That it would put Mineral Wells on the proverbial map. She said everything that I had received from the Holy Mother, but without knowing what that "thing" was that was coming. I then explained my "visits" to her from the Holy Virgin. I filled in the blanks for her in regards to this vision of hers. All this began another series of profound visions from Our Lady, continuing what I had begun receiving in 2008. I believe the Lord sent this woman there that night, to further confirm this "prophecy" of Our Lady.

Only God knows what will come to be in regards to His Mother and this prophecy. I've been praying about it almost daily since I was given to discern it. I've offered many Rosaries for it as well. Oh Blessed Queen of the Most Holy Rosary, pray for us!

One last thing about the Blessed Mother. I believe it was in 2009, and I was asking for another physical sign from her, to be sure once again on what I was receiving. I remember clearly praying, "if you're going to be here like you were in Lourdes and Fatima, send me a physical sign". The next day on a Sunday after the Spanish Mass, a lady from the prayer group came to me and handed me a DVD. I look at it, and it's all about Marian apparitions. My physical sign! I didn't hear a single word that this sweet lady said to me after she handed me the DVD, because I was in shock. To have my prayer answered in that way once again, just blew my mind. It still amazes me to this day.

I knew from that sign and others that I haven't written about here, that I was given to discern correctly about the Queen of Heaven and this prophecy.

Chapter 13. More Stories of the Supernatural

Throughout these first 10 years of my "life", there hasn't been much the Lord God hasn't given me to experience at least once. In this last part of this book, I will share some of those stories.

In 2007, I felt a disturbance, which was becoming routine at that point, but this time it had a different feel. It was something I had not felt before. It was neither an evil spirit nor was it a Heavenly one. It was like it had no distinction, but I could feel its presence. It was following me around for quite a while. It was a distinct feeling of being followed. I couldn't for the life of me, figure out what this strange presence was till I began to pray. The Lord finally enlightened my mind to what it was. It was a soul, that had been Purgatory that needed my prayers to be released from there. I prayed the Chaplet of Divine Mercy for this suffering soul, and when I finished offering this powerful prayer for this soul, the presence left and I receive this peace and confirmation from the Holy Spirit to what had occurred.

This happened a second time while I was at the prayer meeting. The soul made itself known to me with the same neutral feel as the first one of this kind. I offered the Chaplet once again for their release, while my dad was speaking and testifying to the group. No one in the group had a clue to what I was given to do that night while sitting among them. I never told anyone what occurred that night. I'm not sure why I didn't testify to that to them that night. Perhaps I felt as though they wouldn't of understood.

I know St. Faustina and St. Padre Pio had similar experiences with souls from Purgatory, so I knew that this experience wasn't unique to just me. I continue to pray for all those suffering souls in Purgatory every day. They are in great need of our prayers. God have mercy on them!

Another example of God's infinite Mercy occurred in 2011. I went to a diocesan youth conference in Dallas with the Youth Group. I had gone to this youth conference, the previous 3 Summer's with our Church's youth.

This youth conference took place at a hotel within the Dallas/Ft Worth International Airport. The conference gathers the youths from all over Diocese of Ft Worth. We typically receive something like 1500 youths, not including the adult chaperones and leaders. Praise and worship, workshops, keynote speakers, games, and Mass, all take place over the 3-day event. It's quite an amazing experience for the youths.

During the early afternoon praise and worship session, which took place in the massive downstairs ballroom, I began to feel a disturbance. Despite all the joy that was all around me in the worshiping of God, my soul was hurting. I then began to feel death. Something then caught my attention. Death, had taken a form. When God presents visions that are corporeal to me, it's in a form that I will recognize. The physical form that Death took, was very similar to what people consider the Grim Reaper to look like. This black cloaked figure, minus the sickle, was roaming about to my left as I was facing the main stage where the music was playing. I followed his path, as he was on the other side of the many rows of seats that stood between me and him. He then disappeared. I so desperately wanted to get up and see where he had gone, but I was in no condition to walk. This death feeling had overtaken me. I then immediately began to pray the Chaplet of Divine Mercy for the soul who was about to die. The feeling slowly began to fade, but it's effect on me lingered for a while.

The praise and worship session had ended, and the large group of youths gathered, had been given a long 2-hour break in preparation for the Saturday night sessions.

The night sessions had begun after the long break, and many people were all over the main lobby that is just outside the large ballroom. Every part of the lower level of the hotel, which included a dining area and many meeting rooms, were being used for the various activities that night.

I was with one of the adult chaperones walking about, when we see our former young priest, the one who had been moved to another parish the Summer before. He was walking with a woman, who was crying very loud. He was taking her by the hand, and leading her to one of the smaller rooms opposite the main lobby. At one point, she went down to her knees and began crying even more. She was very distraught.

We quickly asked some of the other chaperones and adults who were around, who this woman was and why she was crying and seemingly inconsolable.

They told us that this woman was one of the vendors that were stationed in the main lobby. There were many vendors selling everything from books, to t-shirts, to many religious articles.

They said that she had just received the news, that her husband was just killed in a car accident nearby. That was the reason why that she was in hysterics. The whole area now was buzzing with the news of what had just occurred.

Immediately, I realized that the death I received just a few hours earlier, was the death of the woman's husband. The Holy Spirit, just as fast as I realized this, confirmed to me that it was. The usual peace that typically comes with the confirmation, began flowing through my whole body. The death feeling and it's after effects that were lingering, immediately left with this confirmation.

The rest of that night and the following day, everyone was talking about what had happened. Many people offered their prayers for this poor woman and her family, during the rest of the conference.

The final day at Mass, when they mentioned once more of the tragedy that occurred the night before, all I could think about was that God had shown Mercy to this soul who had passed tragically. No one in that whole packed ballroom of 1500 plus people, knew what the Lord had allowed me to see and to pray for, the day before for this soul. It was a lonely feeling to say the least. I guess it felt that way because no one was able to relate to what I had gone through, and plus I had to keep it all in.

Two years later at this same youth conference, the same tragic occurrence happened once again.

I was in the ballroom during the Saturday morning sessions, when something caught my attention once again like it did 2 years prior. I looked to my left like before, and I saw Death once again but this time, there were no feelings attached to it, which was odd to me at the time. This dark apparition was very brief compared to the first one. It was so quick, that I almost brushed it off. I said a quick prayer, and my focus went back to the main stage where one of the keynote speakers were doing one of their talks.

A couple of hours later, a group of our youths came into the ballroom where I was still at, attending a workshop that was taking place there. They all came in very quickly and with stunned looks on their faces. They said that one of the volunteers that was leading one of the workshops in another part of the hotel's lower level, had collapsed in the middle of the workshop. Some of the other adults in the workshop began CPR on this man. They quickly dismissed all the youths there in order to tend to this man. The paramedics quickly responded after they were summoned, and took the man to the hospital. I quickly began the Chaplet, as our youths continued telling us what had happened.

Later on that afternoon, the news came back that this man had died. It was a heart attack I believe. The whole conference had a solemn feel to it after that. This man was well known to a lot of people attending the conference. A tribute was paid to him during Mass on the last day.

When I first heard the news of his death, the Holy Spirit confirmed to me, that the apparition from earlier that day was indeed Death and the signaling of the impending death of this man.

This death affected me more than the other one did from two years prior. I went to confession with one of the many priests there, and I broke down a bit in recounting what I had given to experience. The priest's demeanor quickly changed from being a bit distracted, to this very surprised and a little perplexed look on his face. I just needed someone to tell this experience to, and this confession helped. He gave me this sort of standard neutral response, which was expected. He neither discounted me nor encouraged me.

In both of these deaths, my amazement of God's Mercy and His willingness to allow me to partake in some way in it astounded me. It always does with each soul that He allows me to pray for in cases like this. God is Mercy!

Chapter 14. World Youth Day Poland 2016

Ever since 1986, the Catholic Church has celebrated World Youth Day. St. John Paul II instituted this week-long celebration of the Church's Youth. WYD has taken place all over the world from Rome, Italy in 1986, to the most recent, Kraków, Poland in 2016. It's held every 3 years now. The Holy Father takes part in this week long event where millions of youths from all over the world attend. Kraków, saw people from 187 different countries attend.

I wanted to go to WYD in Poland when I first learned of it in 2014. The opportunity to go where St. Faustina lived, and where her remains are, were the main reasons for me wanting to go. My conversion started with her and her "Diary", and the grace to be in Poland on the 10th year of my conversion, seemed like Divine Providence.

2016, was also The Year of Mercy, as promulgated by Pope Francis and the Catholic Church. It all seemed perfect for me to go.

I won a partial scholarship from the Diocese of Ft Worth, Texas, to help pay my way. The scholarship was the result of an essay contest the Diocese held on the theme of WYD 2016, which was Mercy. In further proof of Divine Providence, I submitted my essay on Divine Mercy Sunday 2015.
As July 19, 2016 approached, the day my nephew and I were to leave for the 2-week pilgrimage, which included

Italy and the Czech Republic as well, I was a little weary of going. I don't exactly know why, but as we were about a week away from leaving, I got enthused once again. The prospect of traveling to Europe was once more, fueled that enthusiasm.

The flight overseas, as the day finally arrived for us to leave, was a part of that Divine Providence as well.

I sat by a young lady named Sydney. Little did she know as did I, that she was to play a big part in what I experienced in those 2 weeks abroad.

Immediately as the flight took off, I felt compelled to engage Sydney in conversation. She was more than welcoming in conversing with me on the 10-hour flight across the Atlantic. I got her attention by telling her I was writing a book, as she was about to start reading a book to pass the time. I gave her my essay to read as the conversation went along. I was a little hesitant to tell her about my testimony, so I only shared some of it with her but I "knew", that my sitting by her on that long flight, was a part of God's Plan at that point. I just didn't know why yet.

One of the most amazing things that I encountered at WYD, was a deep devotion to our Catholic Faith from our youth, especially within our group of 209, which include many adults as well. I was blown away by that. Their knowledge of the faith and the teachings of the Church were very edifying and inspiring to me. We did a lot of walking throughout our pilgrimage, and these youths to my amazement, would break into song and prayer as we walked towards our various destinations. It made me proud to be a part of this group.

Everywhere we traveled throughout our pilgrimage, I would keep tabs on where Sydney was. The Lord granted me a "connection" with her, it was the fastest one to date. It was granted to me, the moment I met her. It became stronger as the pilgrimage went along.

Our group included our Bishop, 4 Priests, and several seminarians. A lot of us, were able to go to confession with them one night outside our hotel during our stay in Rome. I knew the Lord wanted me to share more of my testimony with Sydney, and so I was able to after confessions that night. We spoke in the parking lot of our hotel during the late, pleasant, Italian evening. I went through more of what Lord had allowed me to experience over the previous 10 years to her. I told her how the Lord had "connected" me to her, and what I could feel within her and the reasons why. She began to well up with tears. Sydney took it all in with great faith. I know I overwhelmed her with what I had just told her. This was the Lord's way of reaching out to her, to help her on her path. I could feel the Lord's love for her, which was beginning to make me well up with tears as well. That was a beautiful night.

A lot of times the Lord allows me to feel some of His love for people, and at times, it's very hard for me to handle. It feels like my heart wants to jump out of my chest. It's an incredible feeling, but at the same time I know that what I'm feeling is not for me. It's strange in a way, He withdraws that feeling of love from me, in order for me to feel His love for others.

I don't feel the Lord's love in the way I just explained for myself. I feel His presence though, but there's also an abandonment that I feel. In the early years, the abandonment feeling was very profound. It was a shock to my system so to speak. Now, it's something that I live with. To me, it's for a purpose. I wouldn't be able to feel all that I'm given to feel, if I felt His Love on a constant basis. I do feel His love though, in the sorrow and pain and hurt that I'm given to feel in others. In their darkest moments, is when His love shines forth towards me.

The next day after I spoke to Sydney in the parking lot, I hardly saw her because of the way our pilgrimage was set up. I went through a separation anxiety all that next day. The "connection" that started immediately with her, made the separation very hard on my soul. It physically hurt me. I felt a pain in my chest. It was like a heartache to an extreme level. I've felt this before, but never to this level. The feeling peaked by that evening. It turned from separation anxiety, to a death feeling. I was walking outside the hotel feeling totally alone. I needed prayer, I needed someone to pray with me. I decided to go to the leaders of the trip and ask them to pray with me, as I saw them in the lobby talking. I stopped though, as I was about to enter the lobby. I said to myself, "I have to endure this", and so I took my Rosary out of my pocket and began to pray the Chaplet of Divine Mercy for whoever death was coming for. I was walking all about the grounds of this Roman hotel, with what felt like a broken soul, and all the while praying non-stop.

The young man who was in charge of the WYD pilgrimage works for the diocese. He brought his young wife and 2 small children with him. His wife, a Catholic convert, was very sweet and nice, and there seemed to be something about her. Meaning, I felt that I needed to talk to her, to give testimony to her. I sat with her and her family at one of the lunches we had in Rome, and she genuinely was a kind soul. I could feel that within her. I found out the reason that I "needed" to speak her, just a short time later.

A couple of days after that dark day in Rome, I prayed in front of Our Lady in one of the many incredible basilicas we visited, and I asked her to help me understand what I had felt that night in Rome.

We finally arrived in Poland, the location of WYD, after spending the night in the Czech-Republic. We stayed at a hostel at one of the universities there. As part of the program for our large group, we would break up into small groups and discuss the many things that we had experienced up to that point of the pilgrimage. My small group was led by the young man in charge. In one of the first gatherings we had in Poland, it was just me and my nephew and another young student with the pilgrimage leader. The leader, who looked a little spent at this point of the trip, told our group that his wife got a call while we were in the Czech-Republic, with the news that her grandmother had just passed away. Her grandmother was ill before they left on the pilgrimage. At that point, I knew that what I felt that night in Rome, was the impending death of the young woman's grandmother. It was also the reason that I felt the need to speak to the young man's wife. The lingering feeling of that night in Rome immediately left me. Our Lady had answered my prayer! My peace once again returned. Sydney, with my separation anxiety that I had with her, was the trigger for all of this. It's amazing how the Lord works. The "connection" led to all this, it led to the Lord's infinite mercy upon this women's soul. I ended up telling this young man about what had occurred after our little group meeting. He understood and gave me some encouraging words that he "received" from the Lord at that moment.

I ended up telling Sydney all that had happened a couple of days later. Again, it was a lot for her to process but she believed it. The rest of the pilgrimage, I was always near her. It wasn't by design, it was because of God's Providence.

Sydney is a unique soul, in terms of how fast I was allowed to "connect" with her. She is a special soul as well, that I do know for sure. There were some others, that I also "felt" some things with as well. Including this young girl, who was also a scholarship winner for this trip. Her story began very rough, as she was abused by her birth mother for the first part of her life. She was taken away from her mother when she was 8 years old and placed into foster care. Her foster parents eventually adopted her. She entered the Catholic faith a short time later. I could feel the hurt and pain within her as she prayed at one of the holy sites we visited. I believe, it's the unresolved hurt and pain from those years of abuse. She also was a victim of a vicious dog bite to her face, which one can still see the damage nearly 10 years later. The moment I felt those feelings within her, I felt so much sympathy for her. I wanted to tell her what I felt, telling her what the Lord had allowed me to feel within her, but it wasn't God's will for me at the time. Nevertheless, she has been in prayers from that moment on.

We had the incredible opportunity to visit the Auschwitz Concentration Camp on this pilgrimage as well. This was one of the places that I was really looking forward to visiting.

As we arrived in the late afternoon, the skies were a little darkened by the rain that had fallen a little earlier. I prepared myself with prayer, not knowing what I was going to be given to feel there, where so many so souls were exterminated by the Nazis, including 2 Saints, St. Maximilian Kolbe and St. Edith Stein.

Our tour was shortened because of the incredible influx of pilgrims from WYD. We were just taken around through part of the Death Camp, mostly in between the barracks. We made multiple stops at the various signs, indicating what had occurred at certain points of the camp. I couldn't feel anything during the first part of the tour, which I found a little odd since over a million people were killed there.

It wasn't until we reached the barrack where St. Maximilian Kolbe was killed, that I was given to feel something. This heroic Saint was taken to the basement of this particular barrack in order to starve him to death, along with 9 other prisoners, who were chosen randomly to be killed, as the penalty for an escaped prisoner. St. Kolbe, wasn't originally chosen, but he voluntarily took the place of a family man who was. This man was pleading for his life when St. Kolbe stepped in. St. Kolbe didn't die of starvation. He and a couple of other prisoners survived that inhuman torture. They were then taken back upstairs and injected with poison, and with that, they all perished.

In between that barrack and the next one, stood a cemented wall where other prisoners were killed via firing squads. It was at this point, where I was given to feel everything.

I felt all of the prayers that had occurred there by the prisoners and by that of St. Maximilian Kolbe during that time. The prayers of those who have visited this Death Camp since then, was mixed in with that as well. It was much stronger in St. Kolbe's area than it was in the other areas we toured. I believe an incredible amount of prayer had occurred there, by the prisoners during those years, when this unfathomable evil was taking place. I believe that is the reason that I was only given to feel the faint imprint of the indescribable evil that took place there. All these things, were all still there in a way. It was a strange combination of feelings, to say the least.

There were a couple of occasions in Poland, when the official WYD festivities began, that I could feel the Holy Spirit among the multitude. My whole body could feel all the faithful feeling the Holy Spirit. I was just absorbing it all. That was an interesting feeling as well. I've been given to feel that before, but at a much smaller scale. My mind knows what my soul is feeling, but it also knows that it's not my own feeling, but of that of someone else. It's a little different from the typical empathic feelings I'm given to feel. To feel the over 1 million people who were all there praising the Lord, was something special to feel. Thanks be to God for that grace!

The other occasion where I felt something, was at the convent and church where the resting place of St.

Faustina is located. As I waited in line under the warm sun in Kraków, waiting to go see the original Divine Mercy image and the tomb of St. Faustina, I held back tears at the thought of my long 10-year journey at that moment, that began with St. Faustina and her "Diary". It felt like I had come full circle by God's grace. I was at the place where the Chaplet of Divine Mercy was given to her by Our Lord, and where she prayed it countless times for souls. We got to pray the Chaplet in the courtyard near the convent, where she prayed it as well at 3 p.m., the Hour of Mercy. This was the highlight of the pilgrimage for me.

It was an incredible pilgrimage, to say the least. The best part for me though, was my pilgrimage group. They were an incredible mix of faithful souls. It was a blessed trip all the way around. Thank you Lord for allowing me to be a part of it!

Chapter 15. Hell and Satan

Some of the most darkest visions I have ever received, were of Hell and of Satan. I have always had, since I was a kid and into adulthood, a deep fear of Hell. I don't know how that fear began, but I have always had it with me.

The first of these dark visions, was the vision of Hell. This horrible vision occurred within the first 3 months of my conversion. It started with a dream that came to pass the next day at a local Mexican restaurant. We use to frequent that mid-town restaurant every Thursday back in those early years of my conversion.

In the dream, the "girl" made an appearance. The same girl, that began my conversion. The part of the dream that came to pass, was her appearance. We saw her at lunch at this restaurant, and she was wearing the exact same clothes from the dream. She also had the exact same hairstyle, which were 2 ponytails that were braided. I knew that this was a sign of some kind, but I didn't know what for though.

I got home after lunch and I was about to take a nap. Our workdays are split up, we have our morning work and then we do our late afternoon and evening work. Naps for me are necessary because the day becomes very long and draining if a good break isn't taken.

I sat down on my recliner and I reclined back and I shut my eyes, and that moment, my soul and my mind and my conscience, seemed to be literally descending downwards at a rapid pace. What I saw, was nothing of this world. The feeling was strange. At first, I was on my recliner and then in an instant, I was in another place, which was very dark in nature. The first think I saw was the ground, which was a grayish and ashen looking sand. The sky was similar in color and look. It was all very gloomy. I then looked around to see what was in front of me, and I saw these large fiery pits, which seemed to be full of molten lava. I then saw these creatures crawling out from these multiple pits, which seemed to appear out of nowhere. These creatures, which had the appearance of these of burnt ember human-like figures, were crawling on all fours. My assumption is that these strange burnt figures were demons. In these pits, which they were coming out of, were also filled with condemned souls. They were agonizing and withering in pain. I was frightened at this awful sight. Just as I was processing all this, I was taken out of this horrible vision, and I was back on my recliner. I gathered my thoughts and was given to know that what I just had experienced, was a vision of Hell. My soul felt like it had taken a severe beating, and it felt like it had been taken on a long exhausting journey. This internal feeling was strange. I've been jet-lagged multiple times in my life and this feeling, was like that but it was internally and not physical. I was really frightened to what I had just been given to "see". When this vision occurred, I didn't know the reason why I was given that to experience.

Reflecting back on that experience, I believe it was for a couple reasons. The first reason, it made me pray for souls with great fervor, knowing what lay ahead for those unrepentant souls who die. Secondly, it showed me how parallel my life was to be in regards to the life of St. Faustina. It was her vision of Hell that started it all for me, as I recounted earlier. What I didn't see in that vision, was the Devil himself. That would come later.

A dream in which was I believe was a version of Hell, happened in early 2016. In the dream, I was in a house. It was an older house, and it appeared that a tour was going on within it, and I was taking part in it. I then see this room off to the side and I'm curious to what it is. I finally make my way into it. There seemed to be people from like the late 1800's to early 1900's walking about. Their clothing and hairstyles seemed to be from that time. I gathered that, from the many pictures I've seen from that era. In the middle of this room, which was huge, were some old antique furniture. It wasn't kept very well. It was definitely showing its age by its many marks of chipped wood and faded finish. The feeling as I walk into the room, became like it does when I feel the presence of demons. I then started to see them at that point, as I made my way further in. There were demons all about in this strange room. They were in their usual form of dark disfigured shadows. They were no longer hiding from me as they were initially. I see that one of them had no reflection, as it was right in front of this antique mirror there. The floor was also of wood but it looked really old and grayish. The color reminded me of the vision of Hell, in which the ground had a similar color to it. The evil presence in the room then became really strong, like it was amplified by something. I started praying, but it seemed I was trapped in this old room now. This room, seemed like it was a trap for me, like I was purposely guided into it by some force. My prayers became weak as this evilness was now suppressing me, and I started not being able to get any words out vocally. Whatever this very powerful evil force that was there, wouldn't let me wake up. I consciously was aware at that point, that I needed to wake up but couldn't. Finally, after a long struggle, I was able to wake myself up. The feeling was still overwhelming me as I laid there in my bed. I started praying this lingering feeling away till I fell asleep once more. It was like this evil thing, was trying to scare me, and to show me, how powerful it was. I hadn't had that type of dark dream in a very long while when this dream occurred. I truly believe what I experienced, was a version of Hell and the dark force behind it, Satan himself.

The first appearance of the Evil One, came in a dream. It was probably around 2007 or so, when the dream occurred. In the dream, I was outside the Church on the side street, and I was helping someone load up their SUV. I then feel something staring at me. I turn around, and I see this huge red massive eye that was just glaring at me. It scared me because of the amount of evilness that I felt from it. It was nothing like I've felt before. I "knew" in the dream, that this was Satan himself, and that I finally became the focus of his attention by all the work the Lord had granted me to do. This evilness was letting me know that his gaze was now upon me. I awoke with this fear that carried over from the dream. I admit that it scared me for a bit. Had I really gotten the attention of Satan himself? The increase of the spiritual battles told me yes. I knew that it was only because the Lord had allowed it. Why? To test my faithfulness perhaps or perhaps, to keep me grounded in some way. Whatever reason it was, I trusted in God's Divine Plan for me.

In the Summer of 2014, that same evil gaze came upon me once more and this time, I was fully awake.

The Youth Group, took their Summer trip to New Mexico, to see the amazing Catholic sites that it has. I went with the then Youth Director and his wife, along with 12 of our youths. It was near the end of the second day there, when we decided to treat the kids to a movie. We were in Albuquerque at the time, and we found the nearest theater showing the movie that the youths wanted to watch. We arrived at this theater, which was packed as I assume it always is on a typical Friday night. We then got our seats in the crowded theater and one of the youths triggered a disturbance within me. These "triggers" became the norm in receiving visions or whatever the Lord wanted me to know or to see. It could be a single word from someone, or a picture like I wrote about earlier. This trigger set off something very dark. The attitude of this youth, was what caused this trigger. The disturbance rose fast within me. I "saw" death there in the theater. I could feel it as well. It wasn't just one, it was a "cluster" of them. I couldn't focus on the movie. I then felt this gaze. The same evil feeling from the dream of the gaze, was once again with me. I kept looking behind me to find the source of it, but all I saw, were the many people enjoying the movie. There were probably around 500 people or so in that theater, and no one knew the excruciating feelings I was going through, which was topped off with the gaze of the Devil upon me.

It was a little late as we headed back to our motel for the night. While on the road back, in our huge passenger van, the terrible feelings from the theater began again and it was escalating very fast. I was holding back tears now. We arrived back at the motel, and all the kids went to their rooms, and barely getting out the words, I grabbed the arm of the wife of Youth Director and I said to her, "I need you to pray for me". She didn't understand me at first, and so I had to repeat myself with this great pain in my soul. She quickly got her husband, and then she went off to get her Holy Bible. I was bent over with my hands on my knees, fighting off these tears that were beginning to win that battle. I was trying to explain to this couple, while we stood in the middle of the parking lot, what I was going through and what I had experienced in the theater. I told them about the "gaze". The wife asked me why I was being "looked" at. I explained very hastily, that the Evil One, with his vileness, was angry at me, for praying for mercy for souls right before they died, through the gift the Lord had given me. These souls I told her, were headed towards damnation, but the Lord's Mercy triumphed. The Devil thought that these many souls whom the Lord allowed me to pray for, were his. His utter disdain for me, was on full display in the theater. The wife then read a passage that she just happened to come upon, and it said pretty much the same thing I had just said to her. It was in the Book of Job that she read from. I said to her, "that is exactly what I just told you!". It was confirmation to what I had been through, on this cool New Mexico night. They then invited me to their room as they were worried for me. I know that the wife, was scared to what she had just witnessed in the parking lot. We stayed up till about 1 am or so, just talking. They were trying to console me the best they could, but I was so drained at that point, that there was nothing aside from

God's Divine help, that could've relieved me that night. I am very thankful for that couple. They genuinely cared, but they didn't fully understand the magnitude of what had happened that night. I don't think many people would've understood to be honest.

I've had a couple of more experiences concerning Hell and the Devil, but they were not as powerful as the ones I just wrote about. The purposes of those minor experiences were to show me that the darkness is always there, waiting for me to slip up. Like I said before, the Lord allows all this to take place in my life. It keeps me on guard at all times, but I know that the Precious Blood of Lord covers me and protects me. I know that Our Lady and all the Holy Angels watch over and protect me as well.

Chapter 16. Dark Dreams

There have been a few occasions, where people have recounted to me dreams in which the demonic was after me in some way. I always find it very interesting, when people dream about me in general, but mostly, when it involves the supernatural. It's always a confirmation to what I had been receiving at the time.

The first instance of this occurred in the Summer of 2010 in San Antonio, Texas. This was the first youth trip that I was a part of. I had just finished my first year of teaching Confirmation, when it decided that the Youth Group was going on a trip. Since I had also been helping out with them, I was asked to be one of the chaperones for the trip.

We took a large group to San Antonio that Summer, and we took in the usual sights such as the Alamo, and the historic Catholic Missions. We also had time to enjoy the other attractions that San Antonio has to offer, like its huge amusement park and famous Market Square. It was during a lunch break that we had in the middle of the trip, that one of the youths came up to me and told me about the dream she had about me the night before. She told me that in the dream, multiple demons were after me, and got a hold of me after a struggle. The young girl then said that she picked up a rock and threw it at the demons. She said that she started screaming at them to leave me alone. When she threw the rock, she actually picked up her phone in real life and threw it across the hotel room that she was sharing with some of the other girls. The noise of the phone hitting the wall woke her up. She said the dream was frightening. This dream made me smile, because this was confirmation for me on what I was battling on regular basis at that point.

The second dream worth noting, came from the former Youth Director that was with me on the New Mexico trip. He and his wife had already moved to another town when he told me of the dream. This was about a year after he and wife had moved. I was in occasional contact with him during that year, when he sent me a text message asking me if I was OK. I said to him that the usual had been occurring, meaning that I was still receiving a steady stream of things from Our Lord. He said to me, that he had been dreaming some scary demonic things about me. At first, he didn't want to elaborate because of the high degree of evilness of the dreams he said. He didn't want to scare me. I was intrigued of course. He finally divulged to me, that in one of the dreams, a demon was whispering in my ear influencing me, giving me false visions. He was genuinely worried about me. He witnessed what I went through in New Mexico, and so I see why he was concerned. Ever since New Mexico in 2014, the amount of things that the Lord has allowed me to do, and to "see", and to experience, went to a level that was way beyond what it was prior to New Mexico.

The final dream worth mentioning happened in June of 2016. This dream came from my oldest niece. My oldest niece has experienced some supernatural on her own. Her experiences are mainly from the dark side. My mother and I even had to go to one the houses she was living in a few years prior, to go see what I could "see" and "feel". I "saw" by God's Grace, all the terrible things that had been done at the house prior to my niece and her family living there, which were mainly drug abuse and of many sins of sexual perversion. The Lord showed me the faces of all who had lived there from the recent history of this house. My mother and I prayed and sprinkled a ton of Holy Water all over the house. My niece eventually moved to another house, but the disturbances for her continued.

The dream my niece said, started off at the store that she managed here in town. She walked through the back door in the stock room that leads outside, but instead of going outside which faces a local bank, she walks into her oldest child's room at her house. Everything inside the room was pushed up against the wall she says. She then hears her bedroom door slam, and she goes to check it out. While she was heading towards her bedroom, she passes her youngest child's room, and everything is pushed up against the wall as well. The kitchen was normal as she walked past it. My niece then said that in the dream she was very scared. Her husband and the kids were nowhere to be seen. She called out for them, but no one was there. She then reaches for her bedroom door and begins to walk in, and at that moment, she hears a deep voice calling her from the living room. She starts to head back towards the source of the voice, when she then sees a tall black figure standing there in her path. She said that figure reminded her of the tall figure that she saw at the house that my mother and I went to go pray and sprinkle Holy Water on. She said, that the tall black figure asked her where I was. She told him she didn't know. This awful figure then got mad she said, and it proceeded to throw her couch across the room towards the window. Soon after that, 2 other dark figures appeared from the hallway. These 2 figures stood right by her. They asked my niece, if she was ready to go. She asked them where. They said, "to go see their king". Then they told her, that she needed to find me. They continued saying to her that this ordeal wasn't going to end. They once again asked her where I was. My niece said, that she was so confused in the dream as well. She didn't know if she was already dead or still dreaming. She felt a burn on her arm, and then her arm turned red and blotchy like she was being burned. It was like her skin was falling off. She then looked over, and there was a regularly dressed man. She told this man to help her. She had thought that he was normal since he looked human, but this man started turning into a huge snake. He said to her "call your Uncle Jose or I will take you with me". Then at that point, 3 shadows stood around her, touching her. Every time they touched her she said, "it hurt really bad". She then called me in the dream and told me that I needed to come over. I came alone she said. The snake then left, but the 3 shadows remained behind. I told her to run at that point she recalls, and it was at that moment, that she woke up. She awoke out of breath and very scared. It was one of the worst nightmares that she has ever had, and something she will never forget she said

This dream of hers was really fascinating to me. The level of darkness has also increased around me over the last 2 years since New Mexico, and this dream of hers was more proof of that.

God is Mercy, I know that by my experiences over the first 10 years of my conversion. I'm living proof of that Mercy. I believe that the battle between good and evil is very real, and those same 10 years have proved that to me as well. Most people are oblivious to that battle, and to me, that is very scary. The main job of Satan and his demons, are to ruin our souls. One only has to look around, to see how far we have moved away from God as a society, to see that the Evil One and his minions are doing their job very well.

I believe that's the main reason that I'm given to pray for mercy for souls before they die, it's because so many souls are not in a State of Grace with God. This "life" has definitely shown me that.

It's a nice sentiment to think that we all have Heaven guaranteed. I wish that were the case, but as St Paul said, "work out your salvation with fear and trembling". Sadly, many people are not doing that.

These incredible spiritual battles of mine, have undoubtedly shown me that the fight for souls, is a raging battle that we all must be ready to fight. It can only be won by turning to God's Mercy.

Chapter 17. Final thoughts

This journey that Lord has allowed me to be on, is something I never in my life expected. All the things that I've recounted in this book may seem far-fetched to some, but to others, I pray that it will give them hope and trust in God's Mercy. I've been beyond blessed to have been a witness to God's Infinite Mercy and to His Miracles. It hasn't been an easy road, it's actually been the hardest thing I've ever had to endure in my life, but I wouldn't have it any other way. I actually was given a choice to continue this path, very early on in my conversion. It was like 3 or 4 months after my conversion, that I was given to "know", that I had a choice. The Lord asked me if I wanted to stop or continue down this road. I had no clue at that point, what lay ahead for me. I didn't want to stop though. I surrendered everything to Him, my will, my soul, my heart and my life. I was willing to go through Hell for Him and actually, I did literally. All the pain and sorrow and suffering, has all been worth it. It's all been for the salvation of souls, to help my fellow brothers and sisters.

Of all the gifts I've been given, the gift of seeing death coming so I can offer prayers of mercy, has been the greatest gift the Lord has granted me. I will end this book, with something I posted on social media in early 2016. I posted it because these "clusters" of death, seemed to be non-stop at that point in time, and I needed relief. Putting it out there so that people could read it, seemed to be what the Lord wanted me to do, and so I did.

My Greatest Gift: The many faces of the dying. My Testimony of God's Divine Mercy.

After 10 years, 10 very long years, I've been given to "see" and "experience" enough death, to last me 100 lifetimes and then some. By God's Grace and Holy Spirit, I've been granted some incredible and miraculous "Spiritual Gifts", but the one "gift", that seems to be the most profound, is the "gift" to "see" and to "feel" and to "know" death coming, so that I can offer up prayers of "Divine Mercy", for souls before their deaths. The promises of those prayers, in particular The Chaplet of Divine Mercy as given to St. Faustina, is that Jesus Himself will show great mercy at the hour of the death of the dying person, and that He Himself, will stand between God the Father and dying person not as a Just Judge, but as a Merciful Savior. Why was this particular "gift" granted to me? I believe it's to give testimony to His Divine Mercy and to show others, that He is truly present in all of our lives and to show the World that miracles do happen every day. I've been hesitant to post this testimony, not because of fear of what people might think, but the fear that the focus would be on me and not on God's Mercy and the miracles taking place, and so I leave this testimony here as part of His Divine Will.

I've "seen" death come with this "gift", to so many souls, that it's been impossible for me to count after all these years. The faces of some have somewhat become faded to me over time, but not forgotten. I "saw" death come for everyone from the 7-year-old little boy who I knew for such a short time, to the countless souls halfway across the world whose names I never knew, and to those few, who took their own lives in great despair. From the souls who were ready, to the numerous who were not. I "saw" death come to every color, to every race, to the young, to the elderly and to those much more in between. It came to mothers, to fathers, to brothers and sisters, to the loved and happy ones full of life, and to the alone who were full of sadness and grief. I've "received" single deaths, to deaths of many all at once. Deaths from accidents and tragedies, to natural deaths, to whichever way death can occur. The souls of each one are ingrained on my soul forever. At times, it feels like a piece of me dies with each precious soul that passes whom I was given to "see" and pray for. It was not great sorrow or great fear that these souls experienced when they passed to the other side, it was the incredible embrace of God's Divine Mercy Who received each precious one. His promises of Divine Mercy made sure of that. I'm a true witness of that Mercy. The pain and sting of all these deaths, still lingers with me one way or another, more so than anyone can possibly imagine. The cries of those who died in great pain and anguish, to those who died silently in the night, both resonate loudly in the depths of my soul. It's my greatest gift, but it's also my greatest sorrow, it's my greatest joy, but it's also my greatest pain. It seems like there's hardly any rest anymore. These past 2 years in particular have been on another level all on its own. This is not including all the other things that He allows me to "see" and to do. That's another testimony for another day perhaps, but it's all been so draining. It's only by God's Grace, that I've been able to function normally, for the most part, in my day to day life while covering all the pain and hurt when I "receive" these deaths. I've gotten a chance to offer that pain and hurt for countless other souls as well. It seems like the moment I'm put back together, the next souls are already on their way. I guess that's the way God wants it. I'm His soldier, so I will follow "whatever He tells me to do". I feel closest to God during these periods more so than any other time. It may sound strange, but uniting ourselves to His Cross, helps us in our salvation. It sanctifies us. There are so many grieving families who'll never know my connection with them. I've mourned with them, I've "felt" their loss. My connections are even with those who are tagged in this post, like my family, my Church Family and those whom I've met not too long ago. Most of them, don't even know that they are in my prayers to this day. I wish I could tell each of them what an incredible blessing their loved ones received at the hour of their death, God's great promise of Divine Mercy. Death is not the end, it's just the beginning. He's promised us Paradise for those who believe, there's just a whole lot of people who need prayers to get there. A lot of my day, working or not working, is spent praying. That's part of what allows me to keep going. I know all these "gifts" are not for me, they are to serve God and others. I use to ask God, "why me and why so much?", but now, I understand that it's not about me, it's all about Him. There's a select few who've helped me through some rough periods, especially when it feels like I've like been hit by a train. To those people, thank you. My hope and prayer with this post, is that those who've lost a loved one recently, or even lost someone years ago, find some peace and solace in this testimony. Trust in God's Mercy. His Mercy is far greater than any of us can imagine. His Plan, far greater than any of us can understand. Something that

I've said before, It's not goodbye to those we've lost, but it's till we meet again! Amen!

Acknowledgments

I would like to give thanks to the Lord God for the grace of writing this book. Without Him, it would've not been possible. I would like to thank the Blessed Mother for her constant intercession as well. Immaculate Heart of Mary, pray for us!

I would like to thank my family and friends for their love and support.

I would like to give a special thanks to Yaretzi Ciprian for being my model for my book cover.

Thank you to Lucy Bustos and Jacqueline Shirley for being my beta-readers. I really appreciated your input.

Thank you to Father Balaji and the parishioners of Our Lady of Lourdes Catholic Church in Mineral Wells, Texas.

Jesus, I Trust In You!

www.ingramcontent.com/pod-product-compliance
Lightning Source LLC
LaVergne TN
LVHW050647100826
845148LV00011B/2012

* 9 7 8 0 6 9 2 8 9 1 7 1 1 *